Thank you for buying my book.
Please claim your free "Stu Heinecke Dingbats"
font at www.cartoonlink.com/claim_font

To my family, Charlotte, Rikke, Søren and Torben, whose love and support made this all possible. To the many clients who believed in my crazy ideas enough to put them to the test. And to all of the people who share my love of cartoons.

This publication is designed to provide accurate and authoritative information in regard to the subject matter covered. It is sold with the understanding
that neither the author or publisher is not engaged in rendering legal accounting or other professional service. If legal advice or other expert assistance is
required, the services of a competent professional should be sought.

Cover design: Stu Heinecke
Cover photo: Creativity Loves Company
Cartoons by: Leo Cullum, Arnold Levin, Eldon Dedini, Gahan Wilson,
Robert Mankoff, Michael Ffolkes, Jack Ziegler, Mick Stevens, Matt Diffee,
Lee Lorenz, Edward Koren, Roz Chast, Anne Gibbons and Stu Heinecke
Spot illustrations by: Stu Heinecke

Published by Stu Heinecke/HMV Tablet Editions
Printed by CreateSpace
ISBN No. 978-0615472515

Drawing
Attention

How to unleash the incredible power
of cartoons in marketing, advertising,
sales promotion, job search, VIP
contact campaigns and more

by
Stu Heinecke

HMV Tablet Editions

Also available on iBooks, Kindle, Nook and Sony Reader

Table
of
Contents

Table of Contents

foreword
by Robert Mankoff
Cartoon Editor of The New Yorker

*P*eople tell me I have the best job in the world. They're wrong, because actually I have the best jobs in the world. For my day job, I'm cartoon editor of *The New Yorker* magazine which means I get to see over one thousand cartoons, every week, from the best cartoonists. From those thousand, I get to pick the best of the best – the crème de la crème, de la crème de la crème. Plus I'm also a cartoonist for the magazine, contributing over nine hundred cartoons since 1977.

However, as much fun as these jobs are, I take cartoons, seriously, very seriously. I have to, because surveys done by *The New Yorker* magazine show that 98% of its readers view the cartoons first and the other 2% are lying.

Now, that last statement is itself a lie, but you didn't think of it as a lie, because you knew it was a joke, which, in this case, though not literally true, expresses through exaggeration ("98% of it' readers") and fabrication ("2% are lying") a truthful insight about human nature, or at least the nature of the humans who subscribe to *The New Yorker*.

Further analysis of this joke might classify it as a certain type, a "one liner" that has the structure of a "set-up" and "punch line. Still further analysis might bring to mind the famous quip of E.B. White who once said "Analyzing humor is like dissecting a frog. Most people aren't interested and the frog dies." Well, he was joking also, but was he also on to a truth? According to Stu Heinecke my old friend, cartoonist, entrepreneur and business humor savant and author of *"Drawing Attention"* he had to be because humor = truth.

And E.B. White's analysis is true for most people, but here is another truth– you're not most people, which is a good thing because most people are never going to learn how to use cartoons to further their business interest and career goals. Never going to use them to make a successful advertisement, email campaign or presentation. Never going to see beyond the funny to the money. That is unless they read this book. I did and I learned a lot which is saying a lot because I already knew a lot about the uses of humor that went beyond entertainment.

That's because besides being a cartoonist and cartoon editor I also founded The Cartoon Bank. Originally I thought that most of the revenue would be derived from people buying prints of their favorite cartoons to hang on their walls or festoon their refrigerators with. That certainly happened but by far the greater use was in presentations, advertisements and reprints in which the message in the cartoon resonated with the message of the user.

© Robert Mankoff

"No, Thursday's out. How about never—is never good for you?"

• • •

An example is the cartoon above, which was reprinted thousand of times and used in presentations with over 100 different topics with titles such as "The Facilitative Leader", "Team Building" , "Time Management", and "Personality Types".

But as successful as the cartoon bank was and is I don't think the true power of using cartoons was every completely harnessed because most users had very little experience using cartoon humor. So it was all a hit or miss proposition with plenty of hits but quite a few misses as well, because they didn't understand the subtle interplay between the person presenting the cartoon, the cartoon itself and the audience. Sometimes the humor would work like a charm but every once in a while like a curse. Now thanks to Stu Heinecke the curse is lifted. In "*Drawing Attention*" he uses his decades long experience in cartooning, advertising and direct marketing to give you the rules of the road for using cartoon humor. Follow it and your use of cartoons in marketing, advertising, or whatever will work like a charm – every time.

Robert Mankoff, Cartoon Editor
The New Yorker
New York, NY
January 31, 2011

foreword

by Bruce Seidman

President of Sandler Training

I met Stu the way most company leaders do. He sent me one of his "BigBoards," which is the system he uses to reach VIPs, CEOs and company Presidents. But it didn't go as smoothly as he would have liked in the beginning. He was trying to reach our Marketing Manager, but ended up instead on a cold call with me, explaining how he uses cartoons to get in the door of some large corporations. As a student of cold calling, I was intrigued; Stu had my attention. But after about four minutes, I said, "I'm sorry, I don't get it. Why don't you just put me through the process you're describing."

The following week, I received a lightweight BigBoard about the size of a 42-inch flat screen television, with clever cartoon on the subject of selling and my name in the caption. As soon as I saw it, I knew right away this could be a door opener for our Sandler Franchisees, so I called Stu back and we spoke for an hour. Together, we brainstormed a campaign that we thought would work in the field.

And did they ever. So far, we have tested over twenty five BigBoards with Sandler franchisees; you'll be reading about some of those results in this book, but I can tell you that they do work. One of our franchisees sent BigBoards to five *Fortune 1000* CEOs; all five agreed to meet and two have already signed up for training programs. Sandler Franchisees are already quite adept at setting appointments with top officers, we understand and preach the value of selling to the top. Even at that, this was a phenomenal result.

Stu Heinecke's BigBoards use a rare combination of cartoons, color, size and clever captions that stimulate people's curiosity, and they take direct response advertising to new dimensions, literally! And at an inexpensive cost to know for certain you are reaching your prospect. We plan to continue using Stu's BigBoards as part of our marketing mix at Sandler Training for years to come.

Stu is the most knowledgeable person I know about the use of cartoons in marketing, sales promotions, etc. He effectively mixes the world of cartooning and business, a rare combination. If a picture is worth a thousand words, how many words is a clever cartoon worth? Read what he has to say and profit from it in your own life and career. You don't need to know how to draw to extract the wisdom Stu has compiled over his thirty years in the cartooning and marketing businesses.

Bruce Seidman, President
Sandler Training
Baltimore, MD
January 11, 2011

by Stu Heinecke © CartoonLink, Inc.

"We're going to have to let one of you go."

Introduction

Everyone seems to have a favorite cartoon, one they've remembered for years. For me it was a nurse answering the phone in a hospital ward saying, *"Urology, can you hold?"*

What's amazing is that I saw that cartoon more than three decades ago and I still remember it clearly today.

I don't know where cartoon ideas come from. I'm often asked how I come up with mine and it's still a mystery to me. All I know is that they show up and I've learned to quickly filter out the ones that don't work and focus on the ones that do.

When they work, cartoons are pure magic. There is usually some nugget of wisdom buried just beneath the surface, a piece of truth suddenly revealed that we all signify our agreement with when we laugh. In fact, cartoons are the purest, most direct form of persuasion I have ever seen.

People truly are drawn to cartoons, perhaps more than to anything else in print. And if a particular cartoon really hits the spot, people often prize their favorites as keepsakes, clipping and posting them to refrigerator doors and office walls, and keeping them there for years.

So wait a minute. Cartoons are supreme attention-getters and they create instant, subliminal agreement and decades-long top-of-mind awareness? That's pretty powerful stuff if you want to sell more, do more and get more in your life, because that usually involves persuading someone to do something for you. Or at least to pay attention to you.

Does that seem like an exaggeration? I mean we are just talking about cartoons here.

It turns out, it's not. I have been using cartoons for the past thirty years to create record-breaking marketing campaigns, meet VIPs and break through to key decision-makers, attract media coverage, supercharge job searches and presentations, and greatly influence social situations.

It's not just me saying cartoons are powerful. Readership surveys conducted by magazines and newspapers over the years have measured the effect cartoons have on readers. The surveys conclude over and over again that cartoons are the best-read and best-remembered part of anything they're in editorially. In the case of newspapers, the cartoons are actually read more than the front page.

It sounds like I've just described the Holy Grail of advertising.

Well, David Ogilvy, one of the greatest minds of the advertising world, certainly didn't think so. He used to tell his followers, "Don't use humor, it doesn't work." If you talk to most marketing experts, many of them will still repeat the same advice today. So who's right?

I think you already know where I stand, because I wouldn't have written this book if I thought cartoons were as useless as the "experts" once did. But the more I think about it, the more I think they may have had it partially right.

Creating a good, effective cartoon is extremely difficult. It's one of the most challenging things I have ever done, which is probably why I enjoy it so much. Odd as it may seem, there are rules to creating and using humor, and if you fail to apply them or simply don't know what they are, your humor will most likely fail. Spectacularly. So one of the missions of this book will be to teach you how cartoons work, what makes them funny and most importantly, what will make a cartoon effective for you. If you are planning to invest in a costly campaign spearheaded by a cartoon, you should read this book carefully, paying close attention to Chapters 1 through 4, where I explain the nature of cartoons, the single most important thing you need to know about cartoons and my ten rules for using cartoons effectively.

No one else in the world has the wealth of quantified test experience tied to the use of cartoons in marketing that I have. Considering how powerful we already know they are, the ability to precisely direct the effect of a cartoon in a campaign is extremely valuable. So if you are a professional marketer or are interested in dramatically growing your own business, you'll find Chapters 5 through 8 extremely valuable. These are where I cover powerful uses of cartoons in direct marketing, e-mail marketing, print advertising and mobile advertising (including iPad and other tablet computers).

Imagine being able to get in touch with virtually anyone. Would that be helpful in your career? I can tell you it has been invaluable in mine. I've used cartoons constantly to reach beyond my grasp, to contact, befriend, collaborate with and sell to people I otherwise would never have been able to reach. Those include Presidents, Prime Ministers, celebrities, CEOs and countless key decision-makers who have made a big difference in my life. And I'll teach you how to do the same in Chapter 9. I'll even provide the tools you'll need to start contacting VIPs right away.

If you want to land a better job with a higher salary, cartoons can help in a big way and you'll want to read about that in Chapter 10. Do you find yourself dreading having to give presentations in your job or at school, perhaps even your church? Cartoons can help you make stellar presentations that are far more persuasive, entertaining and fun for you. And I'll show you how to incorporate works by some of the world's best cartoonists in your PowerPoint presentations at a surprisingly reasonable cost in Chapter 11. If you're ready for fame, Chapter 12 will give you pointers for using cartoons as powerful tools to generate valuable publicity.

Cartoons have never seemed to fit the mission for non-profit organizations. Many nonprofits deal with serious, even deadly diseases, or human tragedy somewhere in the world. Surely, cartoons and humor don't belong anywhere near such serious issues. And yet, they do. It turns out that cartoons have been generating record results in nonprofit development mailings and other forms of promotion, and I will explain how that works in Chapter 13.

Years ago, I was having dinner with a friend in Marina Del Rey, California. He pointed out then Governor Pete Wilson in the restaurant and suggested I reach out with a cartoon. So I quickly drew one up on a bar napkin and had the waiter bring it over. As he left, the Governor stopped by our table, introduced himself and his wife, Gayle, and thanked me for the cartoon. Months later, I sent the Governor a note saying, "I'm not sure you'll remember me..." Well he had! In his reply, he said,

"Of course we remember you! Gayle and I have the napkin framed and hanging over our mantle at home..." Now, if I had just stopped by his table that evening and introduced myself, do you suppose I would have produced the same memorable impression? Of course not. Cartoons have allowed me to stand out in a big way in many types of social situations and I'll teach you to do the same in Chapter 14.

Chapters 15, 16 and 17 will help you get started on your own use of cartoons. These include a resource section to help you find various services and products, even how to reach some of the cartoonists mentioned in the book. You'll also find a special section to explain various ways you can work with my group. CartoonLink is the marketing company I formed years ago to create all of those record-breaking campaigns and membership-based marketing programs that you, too, can put to work in your business or personal projects.

Throughout the book, I will introduce you to some of my favorite cartoonists. I do this for a few reasons, but primarily, I want you to become familiar with some of the very best single-panel gag cartoonists in the world. When you finish this book, you will have become a very selective buyer of cartooning services, so you can start unleashing the power of cartoons in your own professional and personal projects.

I use *The New Yorker* as a style guide for the cartoons in my projects and in this book. *The New Yorker* is an exceptional magazine all on its own, but it is also the top market for single-panel cartooning. You'll find the work of the very best practitioners of the art form in its pages, from all over the world. But the magazine also maintains a style of presenting a cartoon on a printed page that readers readily respond to and recognize. There are other forms of cartooning, including traditional syndicated multi-panel cartoons and political cartoons. While these have their advantages, they are not suited well for many of the missions I describe in the book.

You're about to learn a lot about an art form that truly can draw more attention to you, your projects, thoughts and sales pitches than you've experienced before. You're about to take a wonderful journey that will extend well beyond your reading of this book.

But before we begin, I would like to thank you for buying my book. It means a lot to me that you chose to spend some of your hard-earned money to find out what I know about applying cartoons to various areas of your life, so you can start producing better results.

So I have a gift for you. It's the "Stu Heinecke Dingbats" font, a collection of many of the cartoon spot illustrations found throughout the book, which regularly sells for about $20. You can claim your free copy by visiting http://www.Cartoon-Link.com/claim_font and entering the receipt number associated with your book purchase. Please stop by, download and enjoy it -- and register for even more gifts to come.

Don't forget to claim your free "Stu Heinecke Dingbats" font
at http://www.CartoonLink.com/claim_font

by Leo Cullum © CartoonLink, Inc.

"They've just downgraded our stock from, 'wrap fish in it,' to 'line the birdcage with it.'"

Chapter One

The basics of cartoons

As I write this, I'm sitting in a corner coffee bar on a gloomy morning in Seattle. It's not what you think, it's not raining this particular morning. Today's gloom comes from having lost a good friend, a mentor and one of my true heroes of the cartooning world, Leo Cullum, who passed away just a few days ago.

If you're a fan of cartooning and if you've ever picked up an issue of *The New Yorker*, you're likely familiar with

Leo's work. He was the one of the most prolific cartoonists among the *New Yorker* cartooning greats, having appeared in the magazine more than 800 times over his long, but not long enough career.

Through his cartoons, Leo touched millions of lives, but he occupied a very special place in mine. When I first approached cartooning seriously as a career, I joined the Cartoonist Guild and discovered that one of my heroes lived nearby in Malibu. So I phoned him up, asked if we could meet, and that was the start of our long friendship, collaboration and a great source of inspiration in my life.

The way Leo incorporated expression in his characters, not only through their facial features, but in the posing of their hands taught me a lot about how to direct the characters in my own cartoons to produce great comedic effect.

But Leo was a much more complete inspiration than just in cartooning. He was fighter pilot during the Vietnam War, then a captain for TWA and a consummate family man. He knew how to live well in all aspects of his life, from the way he embraced his precious time with his wife and two daughters to his choice of some of the coolest homes I've ever seen. He was like a big brother and one of the finest cartooning talents in the world. And he was a frequent collaborator in many of the record-breaking campaigns we created for countless clients throughout the world.

Wouldn't it be great if all professions worked the way cartooning does? Cartoonists are in competition with each other, but the reality is, we're also great aficionados of each other's work. We genuinely care about cartooning as an art form and as a market. We care that we're all making a good living doing what we do, because we're stoking the flame of cartooning as well.

I think single-panel gag cartoonists, particularly those seen in *The New Yorker*, are national treasures and their original works of art should be valued at tens of thousands of dollars. Oddly, that is not the case. The editorial market for these great cartoonists continues to dwindle; magazines that used to feature cartoons have either stopped or cut back severely.

While the editorial market may have pulled back for the moment, cartoons are far from a dying art. In fact, considering the markets for advertising, marketing and sales promotion, their future is especially bright. And that is the purpose of this book, to examine the art of using cartoons to generate response rates you've probably never seen before.

The Nature of Cartoons, Cartooning and Cartoonists

Cartoonists are an interesting breed. It's never fair to generalize, and certainly cartoonists are as varied as any other group in the general population. But there are several key traits that set their wonderful minds apart from any other part of the population. If you want to work with the really great cartooning talents of our time, you will do well to understand their nature.

I first discovered great cartooning when as kids, my brothers and I would sneak issues of *Playboy* from our father's dresser drawers. In those days, *Playboy* was a powerhouse magazine. Its monthly circulation was five or six million and it regularly contained the work of some of the best writers and creative minds in the world and its articles really were worthwhile reading. Similarly, the cartooning found in its pages was also top-notch.

But as kids taking a sneak peek at the world that lay just beyond our years, we weren't interested in reading the magazine. We wanted to see the pictures. Along the way, the cartoons really caught my attention. I used to wonder, "Who are these guys? How do they come up with these? How do they create a sense of something having just happened and something about to happen with a single drawing and a short few lines of text?"

I used to think the cartoonists must have been elves, because surely they couldn't just be ordinary people creating those cartoons so masterfully. Years later, when I'd started my marketing agency, I had the great pleasure of meeting, befriending and collaborating with some of those early cartooning heroes. That continues today, with my friendships and working relationships with several of the greats you'll recognize from *The New Yorker*.

When you meet someone like Gahan Wilson, Eldon Dedini, Arnie Levin, Leo Cullum or Bob Mankoff, for example, you're immediately struck by how broadly intelligent these people are. It seems like they're aware of everything. They also have deeply-felt opinions on most things. And if you took some time to talk with them, you'd find yourself feeling privileged to have had them share their thoughts. They're the kind of people you could talk with for hours and never notice how much time had elapsed.

What really makes these people different, though, is how they're able to find those twists, those one-in-a-million exceptions or the singular connection of disparate facts that turns a mundane thought into an entertaining and defining nugget of truth that makes any topic instantly understood. This is exceedingly difficult to do and there are really only a handful of people in the world who can do it effectively.

That is why the cartoonists of *The New Yorker* are such significant voices in our culture. This is as true in the U.S. as it is throughout the world. The language of cartoons is universal and with the exception of a few recent cartoons pertaining to Islam, cartoons and cartoonists seem to be revered in all developed cultures. I think the French really have it right; they regard their favorite cartoonists as modern-day philosophers.

Philosophers? Absolutely. Here in the U.S., cartoonists are generally seen as silly people who make funny drawings. But if you take a closer look, there is always -- always -- some piece of wisdom tied up in anything funny. Have you ever noticed how, when you've experienced something funny, you end up saying, "Hey, but it's true, it is like that," or "I know someone like that," or "I've been through something just like that?"

That is the essence of cartoons. They're precious nuggets of truth revealed in a surprising way. That's it. We'll cover that in more detail in the next chapter, but that's the take-away of this book. If you understand that about cartoons, you're well on your way to using them to great effect in your life, in many delightful ways.

I have mentioned it elsewhere in the book, but I cannot stress enough how drawn to cartoons people are. So what is it that attracts so much attention and goodwill?

I think it's simply because it feels good to let something funny and insightful into our busy day. The experts have told us for a long time that humor is good for your health. It lightens the stresses in your life if only for a brief moment and it just feels good to laugh.

So what do you need to know about the cartoonists behind the laughs? Well, in addition to being knowledgeable, well-rounded and clever, cartoonists are generally preoccupied with getting a fair deal on the rights to their work. It's a very real concern, one you need to understand if you're going to use their work.

Good cartoonists are a rare commodity and considering what they give to the world, they should be treated with strict fairness. They are also celebrities and in a sense, by lending their work to your project, they are providing a kind of celebrity endorsement of it.

Many of the cartoonists are rather reclusive. I remember having a drink with Gahan Wilson once at the bar in the Carlysle Hotel in Manhattan. I had a stack of prints I needed to have him sign, and he was doing it there at the bar while we talked. Not far down was this guy who realized that this was, indeed, Gahan Wilson sitting right there a few stools away. He started to ask, "Hey are you..." and Gahan cut him off, "No."

Whenever you write a book like this, it is imperative that you research what has already been written on your subject. And in mine, I discovered a disturbing trend. There weren't many books focusing on the use of cartoons in advertising and marketing, but the ones I found were written by amateur cartoonists selling their work as marketing solutions.

So it is important to stress that cartoonists are not marketers. They do not direct their work based on marketing test experience because they have none. Instead, they talk about how much fun it will be to have a cartoon in your ad and how much people love their work. Sophisticated marketers know that does not qualify as double-blind testing of new concepts against a control. As a result, I expect these amateurs will lead well-intentioned marketers and business owners down the same path David Ogilvy and others eschewed. They'll pay good money to discover that the use of humor requires a well-defined discipline, shaped by test experience.

Taking a look at the competition turned out to be a very useful exercise. It reminded me why this book is so valuable. People seem to think humor is something unquantifiable, something that cannot be defined by a simple set of rules and test results. But the application of humor in advertising and marketing is entirely quantifiable and subject to the rules I have included in this book.

If you study the great cartoonists, you'll see that it takes a long time to develop their talent, and more importantly, their voice. You can see this play out every week in *The New Yorker*, the Yankee Stadium of single-panel gag cartooning. The magazine doesn't just buy cartoons, they foster and support important voices with a consistently compelling point of view. That is how seriously you should approach your choice of cartoons in your own projects, too.

In general, you won't be able to reach these cartoonists for your projects. Fortunately, though, it's easy to put their work to use through a few services, including my own, Cartoon-Link. More on that later, but for now, it's useful to understand that you're working with a reclusive celebrity who doesn't want to meet you or know about your project, but also someone who, with a few clever strokes of the pen and brush can change the course of your business. It's worth the effort and every dollar you spend.

The ultimate involvement device

Advertisers are always looking for ways to attract our attention and motivate us to act. Involvement devices are techniques used by marketers to make it more interesting for us to engage ourselves in their promotions, with the hope that more involvement means more response. Scratch-offs, peel-offs, coupons, quizzes, membership cards, checks, stamps and those sheets of address labels we like to use even if we didn't donate to the cause are all examples of involvement devices. There are equivalents in digital marketing as well.

I'm not saying these devices don't produce response, because they do. But I have never seen anyone react to any of those devices the way they do to a cartoon. It's worth remembering that the editorial readership surveys support my contention that cartoons truly are the ultimate involvement device, because nothing else captures our attention as completely as a cartoon does in magazines and newspapers.

It's an important point to start from. If you have a marketing campaign, a bid for a job, a deal you want to make -- anything involving persuading someone to do something for you -- the first step is getting their attention. Nothing will happen if you fail in that critical first step.

In direct marketing, they used to say that you have five seconds to get someone's attention and convince them to open the piece rather than throwing it away. It's even less than that now, with the proliferation of our e-mail in-boxes and our frenetically-paced, mobile tech-laden lives. I'd say you have a second at the most. If you don't grab someone's attention and convince them that something compelling awaits inside, beyond the click of a button or tap on a screen, your campaign is dead. If you're trying to reach an important contact or influence a prospective employer, if you don't capture their attention and imagination instantly, you're out of luck.

When you are able to command people's attention, it is an unbeatable advantage to carry into any situation or campaign. I would argue that ability increases your job value by as much as one hundred per-cent, and I have certainly seen it multiply my own worth to clients. Getting important people involved in your deals, in hiring you, in responding to your marketing campaigns, in following your presentations, in accepting you socially is the essence of getting ahead in life. And cartoons can often be a big help.

The basic elements of a cartoon

It's funny, although not in the sense it should be, when I think back on some of the attempts I've seen to use cartoons in campaigns. It's not surprising that marketers will often take the least expensive option when assembling a campaign. And so it's not surprising, either, when they skimp on the cartoon. *"Bob in the back room draws funny pictures, let's have him do it,"* I can imagine them saying.

The problem is, cartooning is a lot more than drawing funny-looking pictures. So when Bob puts pen to paper, the result is likely to reflect his standing as a cartoonist. It will not only make him look amateurish, it will make you look amateurish, too.

So what are the basic elements that make a cartoon viable?

Who's talking? I once saw a cartoon mail piece, obviously done by "Bob in the back room." It had a caption which indicated a conversation was taking place between the two characters shown in the drawing, but neither had their mouths open. So who was talking? A simple overlooked detail, perhaps, but it made the cartoon unreadable and the advertiser foolish for letting it out that way.

Distinctive style: When you look at the cartoon you've chosen, does it look dated? Does it look distinctive, like it could have been published in *The New Yorker*? Is it drawn by a recognized cartoonist? Or does it look like "Bob in the back room" did it in his spare time? Whatever it looks like reflects directly on you as the user. Does it make you look dated and foolish, without taste, or does it show a sense of purpose, that you don't settle for anything less than the very best? The style of the cartoon you use says a lot more than just what's written in the caption.

Composition: When done properly, composition draws the eye to critical story elements. There are tricks to composing a picture, as I'm sure you've noticed when you've taken a photograph. Items in the picture create a symbolic visual flow; the way a table sits, then leads the eye to the person at the head of the table; the way others seated at the table are looking toward the key character in the drawing all create a sense of cohesiveness to the concept of the cartoon. Without it, the cartoon won't make sense. It will seem disorganized and leave the reader wondering what the cartoon was trying to say. And it will leave a negative impression of you with the reader.

Interaction: When characters interact, a delightful friction occurs. In a cartoon, that interaction needs to support the gag or the cartoon won't make sense. If you have an angry caption and the characters are all smiling, it won't make sense to the reader.

Conflict: It seems conflict is at the heart of most viable humor. Most effective gags pit one character against another or against the situation in the background. If "Back-room Bob" has created a cartoon for your campaign that has no conflict, it is likely the cartoon simply has no humor. Bob may have created it that way, thinking that you didn't want to insult anyone, but if a cartoon has no conflict, it usually falls flat.

Humor: It's pretty obvious, but if your cartoon isn't funny, it's a waste of your audience's time. People are drawn to cartoons because they expect to be entertained with something funny and insightful. If the cartoon isn't funny, it disappoints. And you don't want to go to all this trouble just to disappoint your audience.

Direction: Who is the butt of the joke? The humor of the cartoon must be carefully directed, so that you don't insult your audience. This is tougher than it appears, because familiar humor -- the way we joke with friends -- is very different from the humor you need to employ in a campaign. You don't want to position the recipient of your campaign piece in a negative way in the humor.

Are you getting the sense that cartooning is much harder than it looks? It is!

Humor = Truth

The most critical element of an effective cartoon is that it must be true, because humor is truth. You've probably noticed that, when you find something funny, you find yourself saying, *"Huh, but it's true, it is like that."* The act of "getting" a cartoon or joke is really the act of recognizing the underlying truth in the humor.

That's a key point in how cartoons are used. Actually, it's *the* key point, because the entire purpose of a cartoon is to reveal truth in a surprising way. Focus on whatever the truth revealed is. That's the message of the cartoon, and it needs to lead the audience to conclude that what you're offering is the answer to a need they have. That's pretty simple, isn't it?

You'd be surprised at how universally clients and marketers do not understand that the cartoon is the device for getting attention, then planting a point of universal agreement based on the truth revealed in the gag. Instead, they focus on injecting their brand or offer into the cartoon, which kills the humor.

I believe this distinction is what prevented David Ogilvy and others from succeeding with the use of cartoons in their campaigns. If only they had understood that the humor needs to support the truth behind the product or offer, not showcase their clients' brands, they would have seen very different results.

I created a tremendously successful subscription acquisition campaign years ago for *Outdoor Life* magazine. The format was a double-panel postcard, the type that has a tear-off order card with the front panel featuring a cartoon with the caption personalized in the recipient's name. The cartoon showed two fishermen standing on a dock at the edge of a pond. One was holding an enormous bass in his arms and the other was saying, *"That looks like the one <Fred> threw back."* Now if you were Fred, you'd be pretty amazed, but you'd also feel that the cartoon was true, because of the way it complimented your fishing abilities. It obviously did ring true for a lot of people, because the campaign nearly doubled the response generated by the publisher's previous control ("control" in direct marketing refers to the statistical control against which all test campaigns are measured. "Controls" are also the most effective package a marketer has ever devised, so if a test piece beats the control, it just set the new record for response).

So here's what's remarkable about that use of humor in the campaign. We never said anything about the brand (*Outdoor Life*), offer (70% discount off the newsstand price) or subscribing. All we did is reveal a truth the recipients each felt about their own fishing prowess. But marketers are not trained to set aside their brand when devising any sort of marketing communication, so they continually miss the point when attempting to use humor in the messaging. If the humor is about the advertiser, it's boring and it won't work. If the humor is about the truth behind the need served by the advertiser's product or service, it will be extremely effective, because there is a common point of agreement.

There are exceptions, of course. I'm working on a new test campaign for Easter Seals, which is famous for the sheets Easter Seal stamps in its mailings. Over the years, a lot of people have kept the stamps and used them without making a donation. So the cartoon in the campaign shows two women having lunch in a restaurant, one saying to the other, *"I'm impressed with <Millicent>. Now that is someone who actually pays for their Easter Seals."* So again, if you're Millicent, you're going to feel pretty silly keeping the labels without making a donation. That's the kernel of truth revealed here, that you're going to feel ashamed if you don't donate something.

What's exceptional in this cartoon is that we're actually naming the advertiser, which goes against one of my primary rules. But because the Easter Seals stamps and labels are such an entrenched part of our culture, it works. In fact, it could only work for Easter Seals because that is what they're famous for. And I think you can see the consistency in my logic; even though I'm naming the client's brand in the cartoon, it is an integral part of revealing the truth behind the gag. I'm always steering my cartoons based on what the underlying truth is and how that supports the contention I'm making about the need the recipient has for my client's product or service, even if in this case, it's about feeling good about being part of the solution.

That is how you're going to need to steer your use of cartoons in your projects, too. By not being concerned about what the cartoon says about you as the advertiser, the cartoon says all the more about the character of your brand. By recognizing that your brand is not part of that underlying truth, you support your brand far more by focusing on what's important to the recipient, then telling them how you can help.

Caution: This isn't as easy as it looks

By now, I'm hoping you're feeling excited about putting the power of cartoons to work in your life and career, but also cautious about how you're going to use them. I hope you're getting a stronger sense of how critical it is to choose cartoons and cartoonists carefully, and about how you'll steer your campaign based on the truth revealed in the cartoons you use. If you are going to have an employee or friend create your cartoon, rather than seeking a professional, I hope you're recognizing what a losing proposition that is.

When I think about the caliber of direct marketing experts who have claimed humor does not work, it reinforces my conviction that this is definitely not for amateurs. These are some awfully smart people, and they couldn't figure it out. They didn't have the benefit of this book or the thirty years of test experience I have, but still, I have had no competition in this arena for a very long time, other than a few printers who thought they could cash in using "Bob in the back room."

I hope this book changes that desolation, because the world can always use a bit more humor and laughter. If it does change, it will have to come from a healthy respect for the accomplished talent behind the great cartoons that will power your results.

How to work with cartoonists

If you are lucky enough to have a relationship with one of the great cartoonists, or if you need to work with one of the services I describe later in the book, you still need to understand how to work with cartoonists. Keep in mind, most good cartoonists are not excited about working on advertising campaigns or other commercial projects, as they feel it dilutes the purity of their work. And they're actually right. Also keep in mind that if you use the work of one of the top cartoonists in the country, you're actually getting a bit of a celebrity endorsement. If they create something that is clever and fits the criteria in this book, they will be providing a powerful engine to drive your campaign.

So you need to understand how a cartoonists make their money and how you fit in.

Rights: Generally what a cartoonists sells, whether to a magazine or an advertiser's campaign, are specific rights to use their work. Typically, the cartoonist retains all rights to their work and sells specific use rights to a user. For instance, you might commission a cartoon and have the right to publish it a certain number of times or for a certain length of time. If you want to use it beyond those negotiated uses, you pay an additional fee. But the cartoonist retains ownership of the cartoon throughout the process.

Work for hire: You may not call it "work for hire," when you propose a complete buy-out of their work, but cartoonists are constantly on guard against the outright sale of their cartoons, because it interferes with their method of making a living. In general, it is not necessary to buy a cartoon on a work-for-hire basis, unless there is a concern that it might fall into use by a direct competitor. Even at that, you can stipulate that it won't get used for that purpose. As a cartoonist, I want you to know that work-for-hire is a highly undesirable framework for our collaboration on your projects. Most accomplished cartoonists won't consider it. "Bob in the back room" won't care because his work has no value.

Artwork: Regardless of what rights you negotiate for the use of a cartoon in publication, ownership of the physical artwork is considered entirely separate and generally not included. Even the cartoons that appear in *The New Yorker*, which are sold on the basis of a complete transfer of copyright to the magazine, are still sold to collectors as original art pieces. Similarly, if you happen to own an original, you're most likely restricted from ever publishing it because the artist still retains the publication rights.

Negotiating these details with cartoonists can be uncomfortable. Fortunately, there are a few services available that make it very easy and turn key. CartoonLink is my own company. We specialize in creating campaigns that use personalized cartoons in direct marketing, e-mail marketing, sales promotion and presentations. We have an image bank of more than a thousand cartoons by a variety of artists, many from *The New Yorker*. The Cartoon Bank is owned by *The New Yorker* and is an amazing repository of all of the cartoons ever published in the magazine as well as many of the cartoons by their regulars that never made it in the magazine. They have nearly 200,000 cartoons that are not personalized, but are very useful for many of the missions described in this book.

Key Points to Remember

- ✓ Great cartoonists are a valuable resource for your projects

- ✓ Cartoonists are not marketers, so they'll need your precise direction

- ✓ Cartoons are the ultimate involvement device

- ✓ Cartoons need to be constructed carefully or they will fail

- ✓ Humor is nothing more than truth revealed in a surprising way

- ✓ Creating cartoons is not as easy as it looks

- ✓ It's best not to have "Bob in the back room" create cartoons for your projects

- ✓ Working with cartoonists involves complex negotiations for specific rights of use

- ✓ There are services that can make all of this easy and turn key

by Arnie Levin © CartoonLink, Inc.

"Don't put me on hold, Bob. I only have
a two-week lifespan."

Chapter Two

Cartoons as a marketing device

I met Arnie Levin about fifteen years ago in one of the
most interesting places I could imagine. It was in the waiting room on the fourteenth floor in *The New Yorker's* old digs
on 45th Street. This was a relic of a building, with a grand
old lobby housing elevators with the spinning arrows indicating where the boxes were in their shafts. There was a faded
old-world opulence to the place, but by the time you got to the
cartoon floor, it was flatly drab; there was nothing to tip the
visitor off to the precious torrent of creativity flowing from that
modest suite of offices.

Arnie and I had agreed to meet there that afternoon, as this was review day, when all of the regular cartoonists come in to pitch their latest roughs each week to the cartoon editor. I've been to these events a few times and they really are a fascinating hidden spectacle of cartooning. Sitting there in the waiting room are ten or twenty of the best cartoonists in the world and they all look like they've just been sent to the principal's office.

But Arnie never seemed affected. He was always smiling, laughing, carrying on with the other cartoonists and you could tell they liked him a lot. Arnie is one of those people whom you feel you've known for years, even though you've just met.

Arnie's work is some of the best I've ever seen. His whimsical, minimalist drawings pull you in while the ideas behind them are sharp as a razor. Look closely at sparse, wavy lines in his drawings and you almost lose sight of what they are. But what they really are is pure genius on paper.

Like many of the cartoonists I've worked with, he is also a good friend who introduced me to such delights as the Century Club and riding Harleys. I'm not sure I'm supposed to acknowledge the existence of the Century Club. Housed in a nondescript brownstone just off Fifth Avenue, if you walked by, you'd never know it was there. But walk up a flight of stairs once inside, and you'll enter the secret lair of distinguished fine art painters, sculptors, authors, media personalities and a few of the *New Yorker* cartoonists as well. They celebrate their art together in the form of special showings and readings, but by day, the place resembles a fine restaurant set in the ground floor of a grand library that could have been a set for a Harry Potter movie.

Harley-Davidsons are no secret to anyone, but Arnie did introduce me to his own riding, which inspired me to take it up myself. If you've never tried it, or if you've stood back when those motley riders cruise by, you'll be surprised at how nice these people are. You'll find doctors, lawyers and moguls mixing with regular folk -- and a few well-known cartoonists -- and they're all bonded by their love of loud chrome bikes, open roads and good, plain fun.

If you're ever fortunate enough to meet Arnie, you'd be tempted to think he's a pretty wild guy, with tattooed arms and motorcycle garb. The reality is, he's just a fun guy who happens to be one of the top cartooning talent in the world. If you did happen to meet him by chance, you'd just think he is such great fun to talk to that you'd lose track of time. He'd likely never reveal anything about his being a world-famous cartoonist, because he wouldn't want that to come between you.

Arnie has been a long-time collaborator on many projects and if you become a user of cartoons as a result of reading this book, you'll do well to incorporate his work in your projects. He's a first-rate pro and people respond strongly to his wonderful work.

Why would you ever want to put your budget behind a cartoon?

Whenever I speak to a prospective client about putting their marketing budget behind a cartoon, I have to admit it feels silly even to me. Cartoons look funny, they are funny, and they just don't seem to have the seriousness of purpose necessary to lead a campaign. But there really are some pretty serious marketing reasons behind their use.

I always start by explaining what readership surveys say about cartoons, that they get more attention and cause more impact than anything else in magazines and newspapers, but you already know that. What you don't know yet are some of the results we've seen from the use of cartoons as the engine driving response to campaigns. I will cover those in later chapters, but here's a snapshot.

It's supposed to be impossible to generate a 100% response rate in a direct marketing campaign, but it has now happened a few times with our personalized cartoon campaigns. In one case, we worked with an insurance client who wanted help getting their sales reps in the door with important prospects. The reps were asked to compile a list of their top prospects, resulting in a count of about twelve hundred. Each received a greeting card with a personalized cartoon and the sales reps followed up by phone to request appointments. And they reported a one hundred per-cent conversion rate, twelve hundred appointments with their top prospects.

Another campaign produced a stunning result with a simple postcard featuring a personalized cartoon on one side and a coupon for a free 24-hour stay at an airport parking facility on the other. The piece was mailed to an list of inactive customers of the facility and the strategy was to get them to reactivate through the redemption of the coupon. Within the first 30 days, the campaign produced more response than any other form of advertising the client had ever run, including print, radio and direct mail. But that was just in the first thirty days. The campaign continued to generate a steady stream of coupon redemptions for the next year and a half.

Think about what that says about cartoons as marketing devices. Most of us receive postcards every day and most of those end up in the trash pretty quickly. I can't remember any postcards from the day before, but I know I received them. But the cartoon postcard evidently made so much of an impression that recipients kept it in a prominent place where they would be sure to remember it the next time they took a trip. They continued to be aware of the postcard for up to a year and a half after receiving it. Is there anything else you can think of that can draw that much attention to a postcard?

Some industries tend to be pretty conservative about taking risks in their advertising. I would count pharmaceuticals in that category, so you can imagine how difficult it must have been for Sandoz Pharmaceuticals to hire us to create a four-wave campaign to pharmacists centered around a series of cartoons. They must have been amazed with the result, because they were rewarded with a 56% response rate and a 100% increase in sales of the product. The same happened with a piece we did for Sucrets, which turned out to be the most successful campaign in the history of the brand.

So it's not so silly after all to use a cartoon in a campaign.

The mixing of science and art

Cartoons have powered a lot of record-breaking campaigns, which is enormously significant, because that directly refutes claims by the "experts" that humor does not work. More significantly, the campaigns generate metrics or at least comparative results we can learn from and use to predict future results. Cartooning is an art, but it is quantifiable in its application to marketing, and by extension, other areas you might want to apply them to in your life. I can't quantify, for example, the effect a set of cartoons will have in your next PowerPoint presentation. But I can safely infer that it will make your presentation far more memorable and I can even predict that the audience will like you more. They will certainly remember you more. Same if you use cartoons in social situations.

This book is not just about using cartoons in direct marketing, but I am very fortunate to have a foundation of test history in direct response campaigning. Direct marketing has long had an advantage over other forms of advertising in mass media, because it is precisely measurable. Television, radio and print rely on consumer research, focus groups and sales trends to deduce results, but it is impossible to precisely measure the response they produce. In a mail campaign, it's simple. You know how many pieces go out and how many responses come in. Digital media continues that trend, with even more metrics, so we know, for example, how many recipients opened an e-mail, how many clicked on each link within and how many orders were produced.

With direct response and digital campaign results, we get a clear view of how people react to cartoons, which teaches us how to direct their use for greatest effect in future campaigns. We are mixing statistics and cartooning, science and art. And while that will never tell you how to create an effective cartoon, it will certainly allow you to recognize one that will generate powerful results in your campaign

The word "Campaign" is defined as, "a systematic course of aggressive activities for a specific purpose." It can be used to describe a large-scale sales or advertising push or something as simple as an effort to meet someone or to influence a crowd with a great speech. That certainly is how I mean it throughout this book. Whenever I talk about using cartoons in your campaign, I'm leaving it to you to interpret it to whatever use you have in mind. You can use cartoons to create powerful results in a multi-million dollar marketing campaign just as easily as you can to introduce yourself to your next employer, spouse or partner in a deal.

Similarly, when I talk about results from direct marketing campaigns, don't dismiss them as out of date or irrelevant to, say, a campaign in mobile media. These results allow us to quantify human behavior in response to the stimulus of a well-crafted cartoon, and that applies to any other possible use you may have in mind.

The big secret: The truth is revealed

In the last chapter, I told you that humor is truth and that we need to focus on the underlying truth revealed by cartoons in order to direct their effect.

When you select a cartoon for your project, you're going to need to focus on a lot of factors, but the primary determinant is the truth behind the humor and how it aligns not with your brand, but with the human experience associated with your product, service or mission.

Let's say you're selling a solution that makes business meetings more effective. We've all sat through meetings that seem to go nowhere and waste a lot of time, so there certainly is a common human experience to draw from. I have a cartoon in the CartoonLink image bank that's perfect for this. It shows three executives sitting around a boardroom-style table, each playing a sousaphone. The one in the center is pushing the button on an intercom device on the table, saying, *"Got a minute, Steve, we'd like to run something by you."*

Can you see how that would be effective in a campaign to sell your system, especially if each recipient's name replaced Steve's in the caption? Did you notice that it doesn't mention the name of the product? And if it were forced to shoehorn the name of your product in the caption, it would kill the gag? It's easy to understand why most recipients of this campaign would keep the cartoon on their office wall as a keepsake, because it expresses their frustration with the time most meetings waste.

In this example, there is an additional angle provided by the cartoon, because the primary character is asking the recipient if she can "run something by you." Can you see how that could be used to draw attention to your offer in the accompanying copy? As in, *"Not only can my system help you conduct meetings that are more effective and consume less time, I have a special offer I'd like to run by you..."*

Let's try another example. Let's say you're trying to get ahold of someone named Robert who is not returning your calls. This is a common problem and it often has nothing to do with whether someone actually wants to speak with you. I once had a client who took up to six months to return calls, even though we had an active campaign running together. So I think we could say the truth of this matter is that, if someone is not returning your calls, they're being rude and holding up something that might be very important. Okay, so I have the perfect cartoon in our image bank for this as well. It shows a guy talking on a pay phone at an old, run-down gas station in the desert saying, *"Hi Robert, it's me again. Listen, I don't know if you've been checking your voice mail all last week, but I'm still here at the same number, waiting for your call."*

If you sent this cartoon to Robert, can you see how it would be a disarming way of telling him how much he's holding you up by not returning your call? That really is the truth of the matter, but told in the form of a cartoon, it plants a point of agreement with Robert that he will have a hard time continuing to ignore.

In both examples, we steered our campaign based on the truth revealed by the cartoon we chose. By doing that, we planted a powerful point of agreement with the recipient that is very likely to influence their actions toward you and your campaign.

Why cartoons are always relevant

Everything we do, everything we buy, everything we think is tied to the human experiences we all share. We don't like to be kept waiting. We want to be liked and admired. We fear losing a spouse, our jobs, our income, our capacity to think for ourselves. We want to attract a spouse or significant other, a better paying job, perhaps even fame. We want respect. We never have enough time. We don't want to be held back. We want to be healthy. We want to love and be loved. We need to eat, we need security.

Social scientist Edwin Maslow identified the different levels of human needs we all share as well. Called "Maslow's Hierarchy," his theory says that we progress from level to level, based on which needs have been met and which are still left unfulfilled. Illustrated in a triangular chart, the top level is labeled, "Security." If your security is in jeopardy, you don't worry that you're hungry or want to be loved. You respond to that top-level threat immediately. Satisfied that your well-being is no longer threatened, you move to the next level down, food and shelter. With those satisfied, you move on to the deeper levels of need.

These needs and their associated experiences are universal throughout human existence. They are the basis of civilization and the fuel that drives all commerce. If you can reach people in a way that gets them to recognize that your solution answers an important need in their lives, your campaign will be effective.

But there is a problem. People have their guard up. You don't just walk up and start talking about their needs to get them to hire you, to respect you more or to buy your product. They won't let you in and their shut-down is essentially instantaneous. That's why marketers now say you get just a second to gain someone's attention and get them to decide to read on or click or pick up the phone.

Seen from this framework, cartoons are a very logical device to use in any campaign. People are powerfully drawn to cartoons, allowing your message to break through their natural defenses. Cartoons instantly impart a point of agreement at a deeply visceral level, so they are incredibly persuasive. And they relate to universal human needs and experiences, so cartoons are always relevant.

It might appear that I am saying they should always be used in every campaign in existence, but I'm really not. Cartoons have a lot of impact, but by its very nature, impact fades quickly. I'm not going to generate a lot of impact if I send you too many cartoons at one time, because you'll eventually have had enough. Impact is a lot like the flash unit of a camera; it needs time to recharge between bursts. It's the same with cartoons, although there certainly is a fairly insatiable appetite for them. *The New Yorker* is published weekly and the readers seem to never get enough.

Cartoons also need context. I remember giving a speech once, where I was showing a series of cartoons on screen, first to explain how they work. Then I moved on to explain some of their uses. At one point, I showed a photo of a cartoon print, which is an important format I use to present cartoons as gifts. But on the screen, all the audience saw was just another cartoon. It was a vivid lesson that cartoons require context in a campaign, otherwise they're simply cartoons. If I had shown the cartoon print in a frame, perhaps next to a familiar object to convey its relative size, the audience would have seen it the way I'd intended.

Fortunately, context is usually obvious when the cartoon is used in an ad or marketing piece. Using accompanying copy that amplifies the truth revealed by cartoon defines its context; it's meant to help the reader understand the need you're looking to fulfill. The best example I have ever seen of putting a cartoon into context was in a newspaper ad for Digital Computers. The cartoon said something about having to replace the new computer system because it was already obsolete, with the accompanying headline, "Get Serious." The cartoon looked like it had been clipped out of a newspaper and pinned to a bulletin board, and it illustrated an attitude toward computers Digital wanted to overcome with its ad. Very nicely done.

Even though there are caveats, you should seriously consider using cartoons in your communications frequently. They will make your message more immediate and powerful, because effective cartoons are about universal human needs, desires and experiences. And that makes them instantly relevant to your mission and to your audience.

Key Points to Remember

- It may seem silly at first to consider putting your marketing budget behind a cartoon

- But they bring serious, test-proven horsepower to any campaign

- Mixing metrics with the art of cartooning allows us to steer their use and produce predictable results

- Every product or service addresses universal human needs and experiences

- Cartoons are always relevant to any campaign because they're also about those same needs and experiences

- Cartoons are powerful tools of persuasion because they plant a point of agreement subliminally and instantly

- Cartoons break down people's natural defenses, allowing you and your message in

"Stu Heinecke, Stu Heinecke! Must you always talk about Stu Heinecke?!"

Chapter Three

Personalized versus non-personalized cartoons

B. Kliban, the cartooning phenomenon of the '70s and '80s, once remarked to me that Eldon Dedini's art had the quality of fine Venetian paintings. And I think he got it exactly right. It was Eldon's cartoons that once enthralled me as a ten year old boy sneaking *Playboys* out of his father's dresser drawers. Originally trained as an artist by Disney Studios, what always stood out to me about his work was its beauty. I think he could have made a very good living as a fine art painter if cartooning never worked out.

Fortunately, it did. In *Playboy*, Eldon's work was best known for its satyrs and full-figured, voluptuous women. They all seemed to possess a doe-like beauty to their faces and were the ultimate expression of nymphs. In later years, his work could be seen regularly in *The New Yorker*, along with *Esquire* and many other national magazines over the years.

I collaborated with Eldon on a number of projects, including a series of subscription campaigns for *Playboy*. He was always a joy to work with and talk to. When I first met him, Eldon invited me to visit his home in Carmel, California. Carmel should be familiar to you as the beautiful seaside town that once boasted Clint Eastwood as its mayor. It is home to a lot of well-to-do artists and creative people, which is to say, it's home to a lot of famous people. So Eldon fit right in.

I remember him signing the credit card slip when he took my wife and me to lunch and to see that famous signature emerge from his hand left an indelible impression. It was the signature I'd seen since I was a kid, the signature of one of my all-time heroes of cartooning.

When we first arrived at his house and met his wife Virginia, it was as if he'd created her, as if she had jumped out of one of his paintings. She was obviously the muse behind many of the nymphs found in his cartoons. It's the same with me --

my wife, Charlotte, also shows up as a regular character in my own cartoons.

It's fitting that I show one of Eldon's cartoons above, personalized with my name, because I have been using personalized cartoons in nearly all of my campaigns. Which is what this chapter is about, the differences between personalized and non-personalized cartoons, their advantages and disadvantages, and some of their possible uses.

Both have tremendous value

When I started my dual careers as a cartoonist and marketer, I'd just finished at USC and was employed by a steel distributor in Los Angeles as its marketing manager. With the position, I inherited a weekly direct mail campaign I was expected to manage and improve. Direct marketing wasn't yet in the curriculum at the USC business school, so I attended every seminar I could on the subject.

This was also the time when data-driven personalization was just coming into widespread use. I remember seeing people cut their favorite cartoons out of the newspaper, using "White-Out" to eliminate the names in the captions and writing in their own. They gave me my first glimpse at how powerful the combination of personalization and cartoons could be. I'd already been shown how much people wanted to receive personalized cartoons. All I needed to do is get rid of the White-Out.

Of course, it wasn't going to be that easy, as the experts had pointed out in their direct marketing seminars. Humor would have to be something very carefully handled in my campaigns. But I was determined to make it work, especially with personalization.

I was also a member of the Cartoonists Guild in those days. It was a wonderful organization and they did a terrific job of keeping their members informed of the value of their cartooning talent. The Guild often provided news clippings, but there was this one article from *Folio: Magazine* that stood out and changed everything. That was the article that revealed the prevailing findings of readership surveys, showing that cartoons were the best-read and remembered part of magazines and newspapers.

Obviously, those findings all pertained to cartoons that never included personalization. That just never was part of the equation when cartoons have appeared in editorial products. Interestingly, the nature of magazines and newspapers is changing rapidly in mobile tablet form, and I expect personalization will find its way into that realm. In fact, I'm working on a few projects in that area now and I am sure we'll see elements of personalization find their way in. It'll be interesting.

The point is, cartoons stand well on their own, with or without personalization. And with or without it, cartoons have distinct advantages and characteristics that are of great use to marketers. Let's take a closer look.

Personalized cartoons are my specialty

Years ago, I was exhibiting at the *Direct Marketing Days in New York* show. By then, I was recognized as the founder of a new genre of mail, originating from my use of personalized cartoons. My work had already brought me a lot of visibility, but that was about to reach a new level at this show.

At some point in the day, we noticed that the exhibit hall had cleared out. Paula Zahn, then the anchor of *CBS This Morning*, was the keynote speaker and everyone wanted to hear what she had to say. The show organizers really did well to have her there as part of the show, because people clearly were excited by her presence. And when her speech concluded, everyone seemed to want to find me back in the hall.

Paula had told the audience that direct marketing would see a shift in acceptance by the public. Her staff had done their homework, and I showed up in their research as a particularly good example to support her point. She told the crowd, "Cartoonist Stu Heinecke has found a way to make mailings that are so inviting and personal, you just can't resist opening them."

I think that is a perfect example to make my point about personalized cartoons. They are such powerful devices that I have constantly found myself drawing attention I never would have received any other way. The way that I got to stand out at the show is the way my campaigns have stood out in the marketplace as well.

When we send someone a personalized cartoon, it often ends up posted to refrigerator doors or office walls as a keepsake. In office settings, where most promotional mail is immediately screened away, we find that our pieces achieve high penetration rates, because assistants seldom throw away cartoons about their bosses. The powerful effect of personalized cartoons is at its most extreme when we send them as two-by-three-foot foam boards, to break through to impossible-to-reach VIPs.

The effect of cartoons is already supreme; they distill the truth of any matter into a form that is easily taken in and they plant a point of agreement across a broad audience instantaneously. What personalization adds is the dimension of ego-involvement by the reader. Not only does the reader get the cartoon, it gets them. When people receive a personalized cartoon, they act as though they have received a gift. And they certainly do respond in kind.

Personalization is so powerful it can sometimes have unintended effects. We created a very successful campaign for *Forbes Magazine* that became their new control (I'll explain that further in Chapter 5). The piece featured a cartoon by Leo Cullum, showing a mom reading a bedtime story to her daughter, who is saying, *"Enough about the three bears. Tell me again about how <John Smith> made a killing in the stock market."* The "John Smith" in the caption is where we filled in the first and last name of each recipient, but one poor fellow didn't quite understand. He called the *Forbes* circulation department in a panic, asking how many of that piece had been mailed. "About a million," the staff member replied, leaving the caller in even more of a panic. "Why do you ask?" It was all cleared up when it was explained that each recipient received the mail piece with their own name in the caption. The caller was worried sick, because he had indeed just made a killing in the stock market, and he was afraid *Forbes Magazine* had just told the entire world about his new-found wealth in its mailing.

There was another campaign we did for *Scientific American* that featured three scientists standing behind a control console, with a big radio telescope antenna showing in the distance through the window. One scientist was showing another around, while the third scientist operating the controls explained, *"So far our search for intelligent life has turned up a couple of false alarms and someone named Russ Feingold from Wisconsin."* Or at least that's what the one said that reached Senator Feingold's office. As you can imagine, that was quite a surprise to the Senator, compounded by the fact that he'd believed that everyone on the mailing list got that same cartoon about him. We received a call from his staff asking if they could buy the original, but once I explained that only his mail piece featured his name in the caption, the interest suddenly disappeared.

Both stories point to the strong effect the combination of personalization and cartoons can stir. But it grew to monstrous proportions in this one last story, about Fred Tokars, a one-time prominent attorney and district attorney from Atlanta -- and my humble direct mail campaign for *Small Business Reports*. This was a regular #10 business envelope with one of my cartoons on the front. It showed two executives in a corner office with a newspaper splayed across the desk, one of them clearly agitated, saying, *"Have you seen the latest issue of the Journal? It's all, 'Fred Tokars this, Fred Tokars that,' and nothing about us."* The piece was mailed to Mr. Tokars' old address from when he had once been on staff with the district attorney's office. The complication was, he had just given a statement the night before, railing at the press, particularly *The Atlanta Constitution Journal*, for running stories speculating that he was indeed responsible for the recent contract murder of his wife.

The DA's office didn't know what to make of it, didn't dare open it, and eventually gave the envelope to a reporter from *The Atlanta Constitution Journal* -- otherwise known as just "the Journal" by locals. With trepidation, the reporter carefully opened the envelope to discover our innocent little subscription offer from the magazine, and that's when the story really took off. The mailing and surrounding circumstances were published the next day in the paper and the cartoon apparently was faxed all over town. It went viral before there was ever such a thing as viral marketing.

As you can probably tell, I'm a big believer in personalized cartoons, but non-personalized cartoons can also have a powerful effect in your projects.

Non-personalized cartoons

Long before I got involved in cartooning, cartoons had been captivating readers in magazines and newspapers. The readership surveys I quote so often were measuring the effect of non-personalized cartoons, finding them to be the most read and remembered feature in any editorial setting. So cartoons are powerful with or without personalization.

As much as I believe in the power of mixing personalization and cartoons, I have to admit that the non-personalized variety seem to be more evolved, their gags more streamlined and pure. I experienced the difference recently, because I have been submitting my own cartoon roughs to *The New Yorker*. I noticed that my own non-personalized cartoons seem to have much shorter captions, sometimes just two to four words. And when I have tried to convert a non-personalized cartoon, I've sometimes found it impossible, or at the very least, diluted in effect.

Earlier in this book, I included one of my cartoons showing a manager meeting with an employee who is holding a ventriloquism dummy. They're all seated at the manager's desk, the employee and dummy regarding the manager alertly, who's telling the two, *"We're going to have to let one of you go."* I really like how this one turned out and wanted to get a personalized version in the CartoonLink image bank. But the best personalized caption I could come up with was, *"<First-name> <Lastname> is saying we're going to have to let one of you go."*

That leaves us with two problems. One, it just doesn't flow as easily, which diminishes its effect. And two, it puts the recipient in the negative position of being the person who tells others to fire employees. Looking at the truth layer of the cartoon, it's saying the recipient is a cold-hearted jerk. I wouldn't want to put my marketing campaign, my bid to become the recipient's vendor, consultant or employee behind a cartoon that infers the recipient is a twit.

Here's another example. I have a new cartoon showing a man in a frothy bathtub, having just answered his cell phone, responding, *"Sorry, wrong tub."* Personalizing the cartoon turns out something like, *"No sorry, Stu's not here. Wrong tub."* It's not bad, but you can see the point. Generally, non-personalized cartoons are a purer form of the underlying concept. There are plenty of exceptions, though, so the fact that personalization may add more words to the caption is not enough of a reason to eliminate it from your plans.

There is a third type of cartoon we should consider, sight gags. A sight gag is a cartoon without a caption, the entire story told through elements in the drawing. A few examples might be helpful. Picture two sweet, elderly women sitting next to one another on the subway. The one on the left is knitting a cute little sweater for her grandchild, and smiling to the woman to the right. Look closely, though, and you'll notice that the knitting is being fed by a stolen loose thread from the other woman's coat, which is unraveling as a result.

Here's another. The scene is of a city sidewalk with a big sandwich board sign blocking the way, with pedestrians stepping to either side to avoid it. The sign reads, *"Please excuse our sign, thank you."* And one more: you're facing three entrances to a multi-story parking garage located at the edge of a downtown river. The sign over the first entrance reads, "Monthly," the sign over the next, "Visitors," and finally, the one to the far right is designated, "Free." Look a little closer, though, and you'll notice the "free" entrance leads to a curved ramp that dumps those vehicles into the river.

As you can tell, sight gags are extremely effective at making a point instantly and decisively. You never know whom you can trust. Sometimes the solution is worse than the problem. There is no free lunch (or parking). One thing sight gags cannot do is incorporate personalization, at least not without unraveling the gag severely.

One of the interesting ways I have seen non-personalized cartoons used is in magazine ads that are made to look like they integrate well with the magazine's content. I see this done often in *The New Yorker*, for example, and I expect it is an effective use.

In the end, whether to use personalized or non-personalized cartoons is simply a matter of choice. I would always opt to use personalization whenever the medium allows it, because

I want the recipient's ego involved. In situations where person-alization is not possible, I would gladly use a non-personalized cartoon to get readers involved with my message. Sight gags are also powerful and immediate, but they do not accommodate the use of personalization.

Key points to remember

- ✓ Both personalized and non-personalized cartoons have tremendous marketing value

- ✓ Personalized cartoons make the message more personally relevant to the recipient

- ✓ Non-personalized cartoons generally are more streamlined in concept

- ✓ Non-personalized cartoons are useful where personalization is not possible

- ✓ Non-personalized cartoons can be used in magazine ads made to fit in with the editorial content

- ✓ If personalization is available, put it to good use

"Ordinarily, you'd hire just me, but because the other party is represented by John Sample, we think you should hire our entire firm."

Chapter Four

Ten rules for using cartoons

Gahan Wilson tells some amazing tales when you ask how he started in cartooning. He was a student at the Chicago Academy of Fine Arts when a young man with a pipe stopped by one day, recruiting cartoonists for his new magazine.

That young man was Hugh Hefner and his new magazine was about to create a sensation in the publishing world and help ignite the sexual revolution. Gahan was in the right place at the right time, but he was also the right guy with the right talent.

Gahan's work still amazes me, forty-five years after first seeing it in my father's pilfered *Playboys*. I've been at it myself for thirty years and my drawing doesn't come close to approaching the quality of his work. It's not a contest and cartooning thrives based on its blend of many styles. What I'm saying, though, is that Gahan remains a true hero of cartooning. I still marvel at his mastery of the art form today, as much as I did as that wide-eyed ten year old kid flipping through the pages of *Playboy*, when I first became fascinated with cartooning.

I have a great deal of admiration for Hugh Hefner as well. My ambition has long been to launch and publish magazines. I love the magazine business and respect the people in it, but none more than Mr. Hefner. It has nothing to do with his hanging out with film people and centerfolds, but everything to do with the way he built his business. He started the magazine with a few thousand dollars borrowed from his mother and with Marilyn Monroe as the centerfold in the first issue. That was sheer genius, and to this day, when I prepare a magazine for launch, I ask myself, *"Where is our Marilyn Monroe in this concept?"* If there isn't one, the idea gets changed or further developed. I won't allow myself waver from the standard Mr. Hefner set all those years ago.

Gahan has told me about the days when *Playboy* was still a young enterprise, when Hef's pad was still the *Playboy* Mansion in Chicago. They would spend days at a time in pajamas and never know whether it was light or dark outside, as the windows had all been covered over to preserve the never-ending party atmosphere. I admire Gahan for his work, but also for being part of a fascinating piece of history.

But *Playboy* is not the full sum of Gahan Wilson as a man or cartoonist. He's a fascinating, intensely intellectual guy who has lived an amazing life, and truly is one of the best cartoonists of all time. You can still see his work in *Playboy* and *The New Yorker* or a regular basis, and fortunately, his work is available for use in your projects through a few sources found in Chapter 16.

The value of test experience

Humor is a free-flowing, undefinable thing, so how could you possibly confine it to statistical measurements and rules? Why would you want to?

Well, it's the reason you're reading this book. We know cartoons are powerful, that they distill an idea to its core and plant it in the reader's brain instantaneously. We know cartoons draw lots of attention and they leave the reader with a point of agreement you can use to persuade. They're incredibly powerful, but you can't direct their effect without knowing what that effect is. Can you imagine trying to fly a jet without instruments?

And then there is the headwind of the "Humor doesn't work" rule the "experts" use to discredit the use of cartoons, almost as if they're saying it's impossible to fly. It is if you don't have a plane and it's impossible to pilot that craft without measurement, feedback and controls. It brings to mind a cartoon I once saw with two businessmen lugging their suitcases through a meadow, looking up at an airliner flying overhead, one of them remarking, *"If God had meant us to fly, he would have given us tickets."*

Let the "experts" walk, we'll fly. We have tickets.

The list of rules that follows is the product of test experience that is unduplicated anywhere in the world. These are the rules the experts never had, the rules I use to steer my use of cartoons in my own campaigns. When you read them, you might be tempted to say that they're common sense, very basic prescripts -- and you'd be right. Nonetheless, the rules cover the mistakes I see marketers making over and over again. No wonder there are still people in the world saying humor does not work. Those become self-fulfilling failures if these rules are not applied.

The rules are the end product of millions of dollars and thirty years worth of double-blind testing of test versus control, or at least some form of comparative results, by some of the most sophisticated marketers in the world. This is enormously significant, because it offers actual proof of efficacy. Moreover, when a concept like using a personalized cartoon to increase response is tested in this environment, it is all the more compelling because the test is competing with a highly-developed "control." When a sophisticated direct marketer tests new packages, their results are measured and compared to the most effective mail piece they have ever devised -- their "control." The term is used as shorthand to describe their all-time champion.

When you consider that we have beaten many controls over the years with our personalized cartoon mailings, sometimes by a factor of two or three, there is no refuting not only that humor works, but that it is one of the most powerful methods ever devised for drawing attention and generating extraordinary results. And not just in direct marketing. The way cartoons perform and the way people behave in response to them does not change when they're applied to different missions.

So please pay close attention to all of the following rules when you use cartoons in your campaigns. Use the rules and they will make your campaigns work extremely well. They are meant to be a resource you'll return to constantly to check your thinking and make sure your use of each cartoon in each campaign is on course. If you ignore the rules or simply gloss over them with a quick one-time read, your campaign will not produce the desired effect, which is to generate more response, sell more, penetrate top executive echelons, give better presentations, get more publicity, more traction in social media -- in short, to improve your results in life.

Rule 1: Focus on the recipient's identity, not yours. Whenever I speak to a new client, the conversation always drifts to some version of, "Oh, this will be great. Let's see if you can get our logo in the cartoon somewhere and make sure you mention our product and our special offer -- and make it funny, of course." Marketers have been trained to inject their brand into everything they do, so it is understandable that they would follow that instinct with the cartoon in their campaign, but this is a fatal mistake. It's probably the reason why so many experts have failed to use humor effectively. I can assure you that no one will find a cartoon about your brand funny or compelling, and the truth revealed by the cartoon is that you're missing the point. When you focus solely on the identity of the recipient, that's when the magic happens. When you focus on yourself or your client, you kill your campaign.

Rule 2: The recipient always comes out on top. If you're using a personalized cartoon, make sure the recipient always comes out on top in the humor. In just about every form of humor, someone is cast as the butt of the joke. If you place your recipient in that position, you've just sent them a personalized insult, which is not going to help your cause. The trick I use is to make sure one of the characters in the cartoon is the butt of the joke. That way, you'll never run the risk of misdirecting the humor or angering the audience. But don't confuse this with simply paying a direct hollow compliment to the recipients, either. What I mean is, if the cartoon showed two women saying, *"<Susan> <Smith> has the greatest hair ever!"* it rings hollow, because there is no gag, and without the gag, there is no truth revealed. Instead, if the cartoon showed someone with awful hair telling the stylist, *"Can you make it like <Susan> <Smith>'s hair?"* you've achieved the desired effect. The recipient is paid a big backhanded compliment because the underlying truth is, the character in the cartoon will never have as nice a head of hair the recipient has.

Rule 3: The cartoon must be relevant to the recipients' lives. I often tell clients a cartoon must be well-targeted. Reading through earlier chapters, you know that targeting involves choosing the right cartoon with the right message, based on its underlying truth. But it also involves common sense about sticking to subjects that are relevant to the audience members' lives. Looking at it from the recipient's side, you may agree with the point made by a cartoon, but if the cartoon does not relate to some important aspect of your life, it won't have the desired effect. I show the campaign we created for *Outdoor Life Magazine* in the next chapter, which was a milestone in our body of test experience. Ultimately, by focusing on fishing as the subject of the cartoon -- the primary passion shared by all readers of the magazine -- we were rewarded with record-breaking response. On the other hand, if we sent a cartoon about housework, even if the underlying truth of the gag was on target, the readers would not find the cartoon relevant to their lives and most likely ignore it. This is an oversimplified example, but when you read about the *Outdoor Life* campaign in Chapter 5, you'll see how differently people respond based on the relevance of the cartoon. The artistic distinction in the cartoon can sometimes be quite subtle, but its relevance can affect response heavily.

Rule 4: It's gotta be funny. As you might imagine, as the inventor of this genre of mail, a lot of poorly-executed imitations have been brought to my attention over the years. I recall one produced by a printer who introduced their competing program. Their introductory mailing featured a "cartoon" showing a mailbox exploding and the mailman saying, *"Wow another HOT DEAL for <John> <Sample>!"* Okay, so they inserted the recipient's name well enough, but they forgot that cartoons are supposed to be funny. They're supposed to have a gag, a twist, a precious nugget of truth revealed in a surprising and clever way. Do you see any of that in their cartoon? I believe the primary reason why cartoons are so well read and remembered is because they are funny. Readers expect a high level of clever humor and a good laugh as their reward for taking the time to read a cartoon. If humor is absent, it disappoints the reader. If it disappoints recipients of your campaign, they will disappoint you with poor results. A good test of whether there is humor present is to look for conflict in the gag. Most great humor involves some level of conflict between the characters.

Rule 5: Use well-known cartoonists. If you were shooting a commercial for your company, would you hire an amateur crew and actors? Would you choose "Bob in the back room" as your spokesman? Or would you recognize the need to make your communication come across as professionally as possible? Would you hire someone off the street as your spokesman if you had access to a celebrity to make that endorsement? Obviously, you would hire the best crew and spokesperson you find, but somehow, this logic often escapes users of cartoons. It must have to do with the way cartoons are constructed. They're meant to look like something the cartoonist jotted down in five minutes, rather than the hours actually spent getting it just right. I think people often misinterpret cartooning as something which is simple to do. It is not. It takes years to become proficient as a cartoonist, even longer for the cartoonist to find his or her voice, which is only part of the reason why it doesn't make sense to hire "Bob in the back room" to create the cartoon for your campaign because he draws funny pictures. Amateurs don't have the proficiency, experience or celebrity cachet to maximize the effect of your campaign. They're likely to make you look like an amateur, too.

Rule 6: Cartoons need context. Early in my career, I gave a presentation to a business group about the power of cartoons and their many uses. On the screen, I first showed a dozen or so cartoons to explain their nature , how they work and what their basic elements are. Then I moved on to some their uses, which brought me to the slide showing a suitable for framing cartoon print. The problem was, on the screen, it just looked like another cartoon. I learned from that experience that cartoons need context, because our brains otherwise switch to simply processing the gag without getting the intended secondary meaning. If I had instead shown the cartoon in a picture frame, the meaning of the image would have made sense to the audience. Similarly, your use of cartoons must be set in the right context. I think the most important element of context is acknowledging the underlying meaning of the cartoon and positioning your message based on whether you agree or disagree with the point made. Earlier, I told the story of Digital Equipment Company, which ran a newspaper ad that made exceptional use of context. The ad showed a cartoon which made the point, "budgets need to allow for computers to be replaced every year due to obsolescence." The cartoon looked like it was torn out of a newspaper itself, creating very effective separation from the rest of the ad which included the headline, "Get Serious." The cartoon made the point that computers become obsolete far too quickly and you just have to accept the fact, but the ad made a very effective counterpoint in favor of the extended utility of Digital's new line of PCs. Pay attention to the context of the cartoon in relation to your own message and offer. Make sure it's clear to the recipient where you stand and show them what you're offering if it involves the cartoon.

Rule 7: Make sure the basics are covered. It's amazing to me that marketers miss the obvious in their use of cartoons. I once saw a cartoon mail piece that showed to businessmen talking across a desk. There was a lifeless personalized caption, along the lines of, *"How are we ever going to keep up with <John> Sample>!"* That's bad enough, because there was no gag, but what made it even worse is that neither of the characters had their mouths open. Who was talking? Cartoons are about truth, even if it's unintended. And the truth here is that the marketer and their cartoonist had no clue what they were doing. So if you're having a cartoon created, make sure the basics are covered so that it makes sense to the audience. If there is a spoken caption, is the right character depicted in the art as the one talking? If there are two characters, are they both shown talking, thus confusing the audience and destroying the effect? Just make sure that, when you look at the cartoon, it makes sense. Be brutally critical, because your audience will be, too. If the cartoon is to be personalized, it is also important to avoid gender-specific references unless you have gender data in your list and one hundred percent confidence in its accuracy. Otherwise, you will be referring to people in your audience in the wrong gender, which is always an insulting. To be safe, I always make sure our captions are written to avoid gender-specific pronouns -- she, he, him and her -- unless I have 100% confidence in the gender data in the list.

Rule 8: Never picture the recipient in the cartoon. Also related to the use of personalized cartoons specifically, the recipient must never be pictured in the art. Characters in the cartoon always need to be referring to the recipient as being somewhere else, or talking to the recipient out of frame or on the phone. The reason is obvious. If you picture a bald man in the cartoon as the recipient, what about men or aren't bald? Or the women in the audience? What about different body types, skin hues and hair colors? If you include the recipient in the cartoon, it will always prompt complaints of, "I don't look like that. That's not me." If you always refer to the recipient out of frame, you never encounter that problem. There are exceptions, but in all of those cases, the identity of the recipient is obscured. For instance, if the cartoon showed two characters on the moon in space suits, you can't see any personal details, so it's fine to depict one of those characters as the recipient. We've shown hands waving out of the window of departing limousines, legs and feet walking by without showing the rest of the body and so forth, but in all instances, we're carefully obscuring identifying features. As a rule, it is best not to picture the recipient in the artwork.

Rule 9: Use the Refrigerator Door Test. This rule is the acid test. After following all of the preceding rules, put yourself in the place of your audience and ask yourself this basic question: "Would I be likely to keep this cartoon on my refrigerator door?" If the answer is, "No," then start over, choose another cartoon. This is a very real question to ask, because we actually do see recipients treating our cartoon mailings as keepsakes, and our cartoons often do get posted to refrigerator doors for months, even years. In offices, recipients often keep our cartoon pieces on their walls or bulletin boards for years as well. Some get faxed throughout the entire building. That is part of the magic you're paying for when you use a cartoon in your campaign, so make sure you are satisfied that it actually will have the intended effect.

Rule 10: Steer based on the underlying truth. If you've
read the preceding chapters, you already know why this rule
is critical to your success. To review, there is always truth
revealed in humor. Your job is to discern what the underlying
truth is with any cartoon you choose to use in your campaign
and steer accordingly. Most people only look at the surface, at
what the words of the caption are saying, rather than the whatever point of agreement is formed by the truth revealed in the
humor. Borrowing from above, the cartoon showing an exploding mailbox with the mailman saying, *"Wow another HOT
DEAL for <John> <Sample>!"* is a perfect example of focusing on the surface rather than the underlying truth. By trying
to make the caption do the work of convincing recipients of the
value of the offer, they exposed an unintended truth: "This is a
ham-fisted attempt to get you to buy something and we really
don't know what we're doing." Clients are always asking if
they can rewrite our captions and I'm always telling them they
can't. That's because I understand the subtext. They're focusing on the surface level, asking to change the caption to make
the cartoon about their brand, product or offer. And I'm telling
them to look beneath the surface at the truth revealed in the
cartoon and use that as the opening point of agreement in their
message copy. The goal is to have the cartoon reveal an unde-
niable, central truth about why the client's service is relevant
and valuable to the audience.

This chapter concludes the section in the book in which
I tell about how cartoons work, how to use them and how to
work with cartoonists. We're going to move on to specific uses
next and then cover the resources available to help you use

cartoons in your projects and campaigns. Before we move on, I need to stress how important this and the preceding chapters are to your success with cartoons. This is the information the "experts" all lacked when they tried to use humor in their campaigns, so please become an expert yourself on this material. It will determine whether you are successful or not in your use of cartoons in your campaigns.

Key points to remember

- ✔ The use of humor is measurable and can be defined by a set of rules

- ✔ The "experts" failed in their attempts to use humor because they operated under an irrelevant set of rules

- ✔ The double-blind test results my rules are based on are relevant to many uses other than just in direct mail

- ✔ The most common mistake marketers make is injecting their brand, identity or offer into the cartoon

- ✔ Marketers need to steer their cartoon campaigns based on the underlying truth revealed in the humor

- ✔ Marketers must also make a hard-nosed assessment of the cartoon they've chosen

- ✔ If a cartoon does not meet all of the criteria set out in the rules, choose or create another

Don't forget to claim your free "Stu Heinecke Dingbats" font
at http://www.CartoonLink.com/claim_font

"Then it's a deal, but just to be on the safe side, let's have someone take a look at this handshake."

Chapter Five

Cartoons in direct marketing

Of all the cartoonists I know, Bob Mankoff has to be the most impressive. Bob is the Cartoon Editor of *The New Yorker*, a post he has held now for 13 years. He is also the founder of the Cartoon Bank and one of the world's great gag cartoonists, whose work has been tickling readers of *The New Yorker* since the mid-seventies. Having combined the worlds of cartooning and business myself, I can tell you it is a very rare and powerful combination, as Bob's story proves.

Years ago, while sitting among his fellow cartoonists during review day at *The New Yorker*, he realized that most of their work was never going to see any use. Here were some of the world's very best cartoonists, producing a torrent of great ideas, and most of them would go to waste. Bob saw opportunity and acted on it. Brainstorming as he spoke, he said to his colleagues that day, "Hey, why don't you let me catalog the stuff we don't sell here and I'll see if I can sell it to someone else. And I'll split the revenue with you."

That was the start of the Cartoon Bank, which is now one of the business units of international publishing conglomerate Condé Nast, publisher of *The New Yorker, Vanity Fair, GQ, Vogue, Glamour, Wired* and *Bon Appétit*. Today, the Cartoon Bank is a repository of roughly 80,000 cartoons that never made it into *The New Yorker* and another 70,000 or so that have. You'll read more about the Cartoon Bank in Chapter 16, where I tell you about various cartooning resources you can tap into for your projects.

I make no secret that becoming one of the cartoonists of *The New Yorker* is one of my greatest ambitions. As the magazine's Cartoon Editor, Bob is the gatekeeper of such dreams, and there are thousands of people trying to get in. Despite once being delightfully lampooned in an episode of Seinfeld, Bob's job is a pretty tough one. Every week, he must review the work of thirty or so regular contributors to the magazine, plus an average of another thousand from unsolicited sources. Although Bob has encouraged me to submit work to the magazine, it hasn't been until just lately that I've committed to taking the plunge. Most of the cartoonists I know who've broken into the magazine describe a period of a year or so, in which they submitted twenty roughs a week before they finally made a sale.

Bob recently paid me the ultimate compliment when he offered to give me a critique of the roughs I'd sent in so far. He told me I was a very good run-of-the-mill cartoonist and that I shouldn't expect to be published in the magazine a lot. To the untrained ear, to anyone who hasn't lived the reality of being a cartoonist, that might sound like a terribly discouraging appraisal. But if you've ever seen Jim Carey's character in *Dumb and Dumber*, when his love interest tells him he has a one in a million shot and he responds, *"So you're telling me there is a chance!"* you'll understand how I feel. There *is* a chance -- and I'm thrilled.

You'll also note that Bob was kind enough to write one of the forewords to this book. From his unusual position in the world of cartooning, Bob is a sought-after expert and speaker on the subject of humor. He understands it perhaps more completely than anyone else in the world, which makes his voice a particularly forceful contribution to the premise of this book, that cartoons are supremely powerful devices of persuasion. He will also be the first to agree that cartooning brings a startling measure of attention and access to people you might never come into contact with otherwise. Bob famously once received a submission of cartoon roughs from David Mamet, the Pulitzer and Tony award-winning playwright, whose accompanying note read, *"I took the liberty of submitting a few cartoons you might want to use in your magazine.*" Bob's response: *"And I took the liberty of sending you a few plays you might want to produce."* Norman Mailer once stopped by, with his first batch of cartoons, hoping to join the ranks of *New Yorker* cartoonists, and was also rejected. Even Johnny Carson once gave it a try, in an era before Bob's tenure, and was rejected by the magazine.

Doling out all that rejection might paint Bob in a negative light, as the ultimate heavy in the cartooning domain, but that is not the case. Bob's real mission is to support great talent while nurturing the next generation of voices to be found in the magazine and in cartooning as a whole. He truly is a unique figure in the art form -- and in the business of cartooning. The mixture of the two has always been powerful, as Walt Disney first demonstrated, and as you will soon discover as you integrate cartoons into your projects and campaigns.

Hall of Fame Performance

While I haven't quite crossed the threshold of becoming a *New Yorker* cartoonist yet, I did receive an honor that was quite special, given the resistance I have always encountered from some quarters within the direct marketing establishment. In 2010, I was nominated for induction into the Direct Marketing

Association's Hall of Fame. I didn't get in, but the nomination was an important recognition of my counterpoint to the industry's "Never Use Humor" rule.

Throughout the earlier chapters in this book, I have explained how cartoons work, what makes them effective and how to use them in your projects. I have also explained that the rules governing the use of cartoons have been derived from a significant body of utterly unique, double-blind testing carried out by sophisticated marketers. The value of that test experience is indisputable; the experts cannot tell us humor doesn't work in the face of such overwhelming evidence. All they can tell us now is that they never figured out how to make it work.

This is, in many respects, the most important chapter of the book, because this is where I present just over a dozen of our most significant campaigns in terms of what they taught us about the use of cartoons. If you are a direct marketer, you'll feel right at home and this will be directly applicable to your campaigns. If you aren't, these campaigns have significance that reaches well beyond the envelope of direct marketing. Knowing how to use a cartoon to address an issue, draw attention and persuade an audience -- whether an audience of one, thousands or millions -- works the same way across all platforms and campaign types. The benefit of having applied cartoons so much in direct marketing is that the whole thing was carefully measured. That becomes our window into their use in all of the missions described in this book.

The thirteen campaigns that follow are the sources of some of our most important findings, but they are far from the entirety of the body work on which the resulting best practices is based. This chapter could easily stretch into an entire book about personalized cartoon mailings, but that is not the purpose here. We're examining the use of cartoons as a device to draw attention and generate greater results in a variety of missions, not just in direct mail.

If you're a marketer, you know how precious and private test results are. So I want to assure you that the results I'm about to share are either done with prior permission and are now publicly known. In some cases, that includes actual numbers, in others, I will only be able to divulge comparative results. You can be assured throughout that all of the case histories presented in this book are based precisely measured results.

You will discover in the following section and through-out this book, that cartoons can produce startling results, starting with a campaign that achieved another feat the experts always told us was impossible, by generating a 100% response rate.

Landmark campaigns

Before we begin, I want to acknowledge the market-ers who took a chance on my crazy ideas about combining cartoons with mail campaigns. They were the true pioneers of the industry, because they listened to our rationales and made the courageous decision to press forward when they could have easily retreated to the advice they'd always heard about humor and direct marketing. And I would like to thank each of them for sharing the results of those campaigns here and in earlier trade press articles.

So here they are, a dozen-plus-one of our landmark campaigns that helped shape the new rules guiding the effective use of cartoons and humor in direct marketing and beyond.

Ticor Title Insurance
Appointment-Generation Campaign

Description: Ticor Title Insurance was looking for a way to get their sales reps in to see their top prospects, so they turned to us to open those doors. The challenge here is that people are generally not willing to spend time with insurance reps of any kind, so they're difficult to pin down for appointments. Our strategy was to surprise the prospects with a greeting card that looked like it had been created just for them and sent personally by each rep. The outer envelope used a handwritten font and live stamp; the return address included the rep's name and address, but no title or company name, nothing to tip the recipient off that this was a business-to-business promotion. Inside, the card featured a cartoon I drew showing two executives standing at a desk in a corner office, one complaining to the other, *"Have you seen the latest Issue of the Journal? It's all, '<Firstname> <Lastname> this, <Firstname> <Lastname> that,' and nothing about us."* (If you read Chapter 3, you'll recognize this cartoon from the Fred Tokars story as well).

The reps were asked to compile a list of their top prospects, resulting in roughly 1,200 recipients for the test.

Results: The cards were mailed and the reps followed up with calls -- and reported that every one of their prospects converted to appointments. That was the first 100% response I had ever heard of, although we have since produced others.

Significance: This test proved the experts wrong in two areas. Humor does indeed work, and apparently, while being exceedingly rare and difficult to pull off, 100% response are possible after all. The fact that the two are linked here suggests how powerful cartoons are as a device to gain attention and positively influence an audience into doing what you want. In the preceding chapter, I state in Rule #1 that the cartoon must focus solely on the recipient's identity, and this reinforces the point. In fact, I would say that the way in which we obscured the Ticor identity until the recipient reached the inside of the card was an effective tactic, because it created curiosity about the intent of the message. You will notice that the cartoon follows Rule #1 precisely, by paying a great compliment to the reader while focusing solely on their identity, not on the client's brand.

Advertising Age/Sales & Marketing Management Subscription Acquisition Campaigns

Description: I include both campaigns together because they were similar in mission and execution. Both were subscription acquisition campaigns for trade magazines, both were required to break through the clutter of mail arriving in busy offices and both had to actually reach the intended recipient without being screened away by assistants. The formats used in the two campaigns were identical, using a standard business size #10 outer envelope, featuring a personalized cartoon and what looked like hand-typed address blocks. Inside was a two-page letter, order card and business reply envelope. Also included was a buck slip amplifying the offer of a free 8" x 10" print of the cartoon with paid order. The Leo Cullum-penned cartoon for the *Advertising Age* piece showed a group of executives in a meeting, one telling the group, *"We need someone with vision, creativity and great marketing instincts... someone like*

<Firstname> <Lastname>." And you'll recognize the cartoon for the *Sales & Marketing Management* campaign from the Ticor case history above.

Results: The *Advertising Age* campaign brought the highest gross response the magazine had seen within the past four years, and the all-time record for cash with order. The *Sales & Marketing Management* test generated nearly three times the response produced by the control, setting a new record for the magazine, for the biggest jump in response produced by a test versus control contest.

Significance: The sad fact for most business-to-business campaigns is that most promotional mail never makes it to the intended recipient. These tests showed that cartoons are supremely powerful devices not only for drawing attention and instant involvement from recipients, but for creating powerful penetration in office settings. As a result of these and other campaigns, we know that assistants rarely throw away cartoons about their bosses, and will often burst in and announce cartoon mail pieces. I think it was also significant that the cartoons are by recognized cartoonists. My work may not be in *The New Yorker* yet, but it has received a lot of exposure over the years and is generally recognized by readers. Leo Cullum was the most prolific cartoonist in the history of *The New Yorker*, having more cartoons appear in the magazine than any other cartoonist. I believe the recognition factor also helped in the push to have support staff view the cartoon as something their bosses needed to see.

Outdoor Life Magazine
Subscription Acquisition Campaign

Description: We were called in to improve upon the current control piece, a double-panel postcard that offered a set of four wildlife prints upon receipt of paid order. At the time, the magazine wasn't sure whether their audience would be more responsive to hunting or fishing themes, so we produced two side-by-side test pieces using cartoons by Leo Cullum. The hunting-oriented piece featured a cartoon showing two hunters walking down a dirt road with group of ducks walking ahead with their wings in the air as if they were now prisoners. One of the hunters explains to the other, *"It's just a little trick I learned from <Firstname> <Lastname>."* The fishing cartoon showed two fishermen standing on a dock, one with an enormous bass in his arms, the other saying, *"That looks like the one <Firstname> <Lastname> threw back."* Both test pieces offered a free 8" x 10" framable print of the respective cartoons.

Results: Both campaigns outperformed the control, with the hunting version generating a 36% increase in front-end response and the fishing cartoon a 65% jump. The fishing version was clearly the winner, also having produced a 78% increase in paid orders over the previous control.

Significance: This is one of the campaigns I often point to when explaining the importance of focusing on the identity of the recipient rather than using the cartoon as a branding device. Neither cartoon mentions the magazine, offer or anything remotely related to subscribing to the magazine, yet this test nearly doubled the response brought by the previous control. I've stated it elsewhere in this book, but I'll emphasize again the significance of beating any direct marketing control. Direct marketing at this level always involves double-blind testing of new packages against a statistical control, in this case, the most effective thing the magazine has ever mailed. If your test piece ties the control, you have just equalled their all-time best mailing; if you beat it, you own the new record. It is quite rare to beat a control by more than a few percentage points; the power of cartoons drove this much higher. It is also worth noting the difference in response rates between the two cartoon versions. We discovered that the *Outdoor Life* audience was indeed more responsive to fishing rather than hunting themes, but we also saw a big difference in results between two seemingly equal cartoons. As you might expect, the better the cartoon, the tighter the underlying concept, and the better the cartoon will perform in your campaign. It makes a strong argument for using the very best talent possible when creating or choosing a cartoon. This is why I constantly rail against hiring "Bob in the back room" because he draws funny pictures, or against hiring inexperienced cartoonists or worse yet, simple illustrators to create your cartoon.

The New Yorker
Subscription Acquisition Campaign

Description: The magazine had already scored a win -- and new control -- by imitating the campaigns I was creating for other magazines. Oddly, they did it while breaking one of my prime directives: don't focus on your brand or offer in the cartoon. I approached the magazine, told them I could beat their control because it was breaking one of my rules and they bought in. Their previous control took form as a double-panel postcard (one half tears off and is used as the business-reply order card), with a cartoon showing an editor bursting in the door of a newsroom, shouting, *"Wait, stop the presses! We have a great subscription offer for <Firstname> <Lastname>!"* I knew recipients would be far more captivated by a piece that simply cast them in a typical *New Yorker* cartoon, with no agenda concerning selling subscriptions. I wanted a pure test, so nothing else was changed in our test piece other than the cartoon. Featured was one of Bob Mankoff's cartoons showing an executive on the phone standing at his desk, looking through his appointment diary, telling the caller, *"No, Thursday's out, <Firstname>. How about never -- is never good for you?"*

Results: Our test beat the previous control, becoming *The New Yorker*'s new control.

Significance: This was a pure test of cartoon versus cartoon, following the rules versus not. Because of that, it provided clear proof that cartoons work best when brand and offer are kept out. It's also a fascinating look into the exceptional relationship the magazine has with its readers, stemming in large part from their love of the cartoons within. I believe the readers were so loyal and so fond of the cartoons in the magazine that they simply looked past the fact that the earlier cartoon was about a subscription offer. In my version, they clearly appreciated the honor of appearing in a real live *New Yorker* cartoon, and showed it by subscribing in larger numbers. This is a difficult point to convince new clients of; they're so insecure about omitting their brand from every element of their campaigns that they miss the opportunity to boost results instead. Given the choice, I'll always opt for more response, but the fact is, leaving your brand out of the cartoon also seems to come across as generosity to the audience. Paradoxically, it enhances your brand.

Restaurant & Hotel Design, Subscriber Acquisition Campaign
Harvard Business Review, Subscriber Copy Delivery On-sert

Description: At first glance, these look like two completely different campaigns -- and obviously, they are. But they are also closely related. The *Restaurant & Hotel Design* piece was sent to architects to get them to sign up for a controlled-circulation offer (the subscription is free, but you must qualify based on completing a questionnaire). The *Harvard Business Review* piece was placed atop roughly 300,000 subscriber copies as the delivery device for that month's issue. What the two had in common was that they both sold framable prints of the featured cartoons as a way to buy-down the cost of the promotion. The *R&HD* piece was a 6" x 9" double-window outer envelope containing a letter, buck slip, qualifying questionnaire and business reply envelope. Also included was an order form to purchase a print of the cartoon for $24.95. The featured cartoon was by Leo Cullum, showing a psychiatrist telling his patient, *"Comparing your designs to <Firstname> <Lastname>'s is not helping your self-esteem."* The *Harvard*

Business Review piece also featured a cartoon by Leo, showing two executives seated across from one another at a desk, with a sales chart on the wall reflecting rising success. One executive was saying to his visitor, *"I can't take all the credit, but it was my decision to hire <Firstname> <Lastname>."* The on-sert included teaser copy about the stories in the enclosed issue and a form to order 11" x 14" signed prints of the personalized cartoon. Five price points were tested for the prints, from $25 to $125, in $25 increments.

Results: *The Restaurant & Hotel Design* campaign netted a very strong 17% response to the subscription offer and produced roughly $3,000 in shared print sale revenue. The *Harvard Business Review* piece produced an astounding $70,000 worth of print sales; all price points sold well, but the winning price was $25. If all five test panels had featured the $25 price point, total print sales would have risen to $90,000.

Significance: In direct marketing, double-blind testing of test versus control is governed by two variables: raw response and cost per order. In the cases above, I have focused only on comparative response, but I have always believed it is possible to produce a zero-cost campaign. If that were to happen, it would disrupt the practice of measuring response against other controls, because those always involve an actual cost for each order generated. In these two tests, we came awfully close to my goal. In the *R&HD* campaign, a 17% response was already a breakthrough. But the publisher had never experienced having a vendor return to present a ceremonial check (a big photo pop) for $1,500 toward reducing the cost of the campaign.

On the *Harvard Business Review* campaign, we generated a $35,000 rebate on their delivery of subscriber copies, which could have reached $45,000 if we had used the winning price point. That really did come close to eliminating the cost of delivering that month's subscriber issues, but more importantly, I think this is a clear demonstration of the way people respond to personalized cartoons. There is no equivalent throughout direct marketing; there is nothing else that appears on envelopes that recipients would pay to receive as a suitable-for-framing print.

Metaprel/Sucrets
Awareness Campaigns

Description: Again, these are two rather different campaigns, but with a common purpose in mind and similarly extraordinary outcomes. Metaprel was a generic version of the brand-name prescriptive drug, Alupent, which had just come off patent. The campaign stretched across four waves, with the goal of encouraging pharmacists to participate in informational installments, designed to explain that Metaprel was the same formulation but half the cost of the market leader. The client hoped to influence pharmacists to intervene when customers walked in with prescriptions for Alupent and recommend Metaprel instead. Each of the four waves of the mailing featured a different cartoon, each part of a four-piece set of prints the pharmacists could collect by responding throughout the campaign. By comparison, the Sucrets campaign was pretty simple, comprised of a 9" x 12" outer envelope with a large window, displaying a print of a cartoon by Gahan Wilson.

The cartoon showed a miserable patient in a doctor's waiting room, speaking to the nurse who is saying, *"Don't you worry, Mr. Kranitz, Doctor <Lastname> will give that streptococcus of yours the old one-two!"* Mailed during cold season, the campaign was designed to raise awareness of the Sucrets brand among general practitioners, with a response device inside they could use to request patient samples.

Results: Although we didn't hear the actual numbers for the Sucrets campaign, it was deemed, "The most successful campaign ever in the history of the brand" by the client, GSK GlaxoSmithKline. The Metaprel campaign produced a 56% front-end response and doubled overall sales of the product. Oddly, after doubling their sales that year, their agency decided to run a different campaign the following year, saying, "the cartoon no longer fits our strategy." I will never understand the logic of that decision.

Significance: There are so many lessons drawn from these two campaigns. I often hear clients voice concern about whether their audience is too sophisticated for cartoons to be effective, but judging from these two campaigns, plus those for *The New Yorker* and other professional audiences represented in this handful of case histories, that clearly is not the case. People are people, whether they are doctors or pharmacists, or fishing aficionados. These campaigns in the aggregate support my contention that cartoons are always relevant, assuming they're targeted properly. Doctors are among the toughest audiences to break through to, and cartoons did the job quite effectively. I still hear stories today, more than fifteen years after this campaign, that pharmacists have prints displayed in their pharmacies from the Metaprel campaign. I have no idea what their agency brought them the following years, but clearly this had staying power. It would have paid off in a big way to have continued the campaign for years, because this and other campaigns have made it clear that cartoons have the ability to engage the audience over multiple touches without diminishing response.

ArthritisToday/**American Diabetes Association**

Description: Here are two more seemingly unrelated campaigns. On the one hand, we have a self-mailer seeking new donors for the American Diabetes Association and a renewal on-sert for the Arthritis Foundation, placed on last issues of their member magazine, *Arthritis Today*. The ADA piece is newer and experimental, using a multi-panel cartoon drawn by me, using a font of my chicken-scratch handwriting to personalize within the caption bubbles. The cartoon shows a couple walking down a sidewalk past a new modern building, the man saying in the first panel, *"Wow, is that the new <Firstname> <Lastname> Research Wing?"* The man continues in the next panel, *"Someday, I want to make a difference like that."*

In the third panel, the woman responds, *"You mean you haven't yet?"* And in the final panel, the man explains, *"I guess I just haven't received the right thing in the mail yet."* When the front panel is lifted, the headline inside reads, "If you want to make a difference, you just received the right thing in the mail." The package also included a temporary membership card filled out in the recipient's name. The piece forms a pouch inside which housed a letter, donation form and business reply card. The Arthritis Foundation piece featured a cartoon showing three scientists taking turns looking through a microscope, one telling the others, *"You'd better get <Firstname> <Lastname> down here right away. That's the darnedest little teeny weeny squiggly thing I've ever seen."* The headline reads, "A member of our team is missing," while the copy continues to tell the lapsing member that they're still needed on the team to defeat the disease.

Results: The Arthritis Foundation on-sert served as control for more than ten years; results unknown for ADA campaign

Significance: "Wait," you're probably thinking, "you count a campaign for which you don't have results among your most pivotal?" Absolutely, and here's why. For years, I've heard people make assumptions about what kinds of missions cartoons are and are not suited for. I have even fallen into that trap, but cartoons have shown me the way out. What's significant about this pair of campaigns is what they show about cartoons always being relevant to the entire spectrum of human experiences -- and still being effective persuasion devices, even when the subject matter is as serious as debilitating and deadly diseases. By focusing on the underlying truth about these diseases, that we all want to do our part to eliminate them, cartoons are still enormously relevant and useful. The performance of the Arthritis Foundation piece proves that point; the diabetes piece, even without results, lights the way even further.

Standard Parking

"I don't recall clearing Jane Sample to land -- or park."

Description: Standard Parking managed a parking facility adjacent to Los Angeles International Airport; they approached us to create a postcard campaign designed to reactivate lapsed customers. The postcards featured a cartoon by me, showing a car parked atop the LAX control tower, with two controllers looking toward the roof, one saying, *"I don't recall clearing <Firstname> <Lastname> to land or park."* The back of the postcard doubled as a coupon for a free 24-hour stay at the facility.

Results: Within the first thirty days, the postcard produced so many coupon redemptions that the client reported this was the most successful campaign they had ever launched in any medium, including television, radio, print and of course, direct mail. After setting that record, the campaign continued to produce a steady stream of coupon redemptions for the next year and a half.

Significance: Most postcards are thrown away immediately, none certainly are memorable beyond a minute or two -- yet our personalized cartoon postcards seem to defy the laws of gravity. Recipients often treat our mailings, especially post-cards, as keepsakes, posting them to refrigerator doors or other memory-wall locations around the house or office. In this case, that "refrigerator door" effect produced an extreme result, because it helped create lasting top-of-mind awareness suffi-cient to remind recipients to use the coupon for their next trip, up to a year and a half after receiving the mail piece. That is an extraordinary result that just would not have been possible without the effect of the personalized cartoon in the piece.

**Best Roofing
Drip/Awareness Campaign**

Description: Roofers have a tough job up on the roof and in their marketing. For the most part, once you've installed a roof, your customers don't need you for another twenty five years. Well, actually, they do, but they don't realize it until a problem occurs. It is a challenge that is impervious to most conventional marketing methods; you can't stimulate demand with coupons, for example. So we devised a monthly drip campaign instead for Best Roofing, that served as a constant reminder that they were there, ready to help when the roof leaked. Our goal was to get property owners and managers to collect the monthly postcards on their walls and reach for them instead of the Yellow Pages or to run a Google search; if the relationship already existed and was freshly on the top of the recipient's mind, we knew Best Roofing would get the call.

Results: Best Roofing's sales soared by 150% over the three-year period of the campaign; one postcard brought in a

$1.3 million sale all on its own, the biggest response I've ever heard of from a single postcard. Many recipients were found to have collected the entire series of thirty six postcards on their walls during the campaign.

Significance: Postcards are often thought of as the runts of the direct marketing world, but they're really quite powerful and one of my favorite formats. They're already open, so their effect is not obscured by an outer envelope, and they're all ready to go up on refrigerator doors or office walls. The combination of personalized cartoons and the postcard format seems to invite recipients to collect the whole series, creating a dialog with the audience and dominant top-of-mind awareness. This campaign proved how powerful that effect could be over a long and frequent campaign. People apparently do not tire of receiving cartoons about themselves, and the drip strategy combination proved to be a big winner.

Uses and formats

Postcards: In the U.S., if the size is 6" x 4.25" or less, special postal rates apply, making this format more affordable. Jumbo postcard sizes are also available. In any size, postcards are a convenient format for featuring a cartoon; if it resonates with the audience members, they will keep postcards on refrigerator doors and office walls, where they can generate months, even years of bonus frequency and exposure of your offer.

Multi-Panel Postcards: These formats are useful when you're asking recipients to separate one panel to send it back as an order. Cartoons are very effective on these pieces, used as the hook on the front panel, perhaps also as a free gift upon paid order. If kept under 6" x 4.25" in the U.S., these pieces also qualify for lower postcard postal rates. The chief disadvantage of this format is that it is not possible to receive cash with order; you cannot ask respondents to write their credit card number on an exposed business reply card.

#10 OE with Matching Letter: There is an argument to be made that business correspondence still comes in the form of a standard #10 business envelope with a letter inside, although I would say e-mail has probably become the new standard. Still, it makes a nice, neat package with a personalized cartoon on the outer envelope and on the letter inside, with matched personalization throughout. This format is subject to letter rates, which have become quite high, but it is still a way to stand out to an executive audience.

Self-Mailers: While this category can include a lot of formats, I want to pay special attention to the amazing innovations developed by R.R. Donnelly. Among those is a special new format called the "comfortable package." It is a tri-fold piece that forms a full-size front flap that opens upward to reveal a lot of space inside for messaging, a pouch containing letter and other elements. One of my favorite aspects of this format it the reveal it creates for the affixed membership or gift card element that attaches to the front of the inner pouch. For reference, this is the format I used for the American Diabetes Association mailing above.

Snap-Packs: Snap-packs are formed by binding multiple plies at either end, forming what looks something like a small #10 envelope. The bound ends sometimes have lines of holes punched along either end to connote old computer rollers. With or without the holes, the right hand side of the bound bundle is perforated to allow recipients to tear it off, leaving a small booklet of elements. Although I didn't show it here, this is the format I used to create the new control for *Forbes Magazine*; it is a viable format that affords multiple personalized elements while curbing the cost of the mailing. This is a highly versatile format that can include, among other things, a full business reply envelope, allowing cash-with-order responses.

Exotics/Experimentals: These could take any form, but there are two that come to mind immediately. I have always been fascinated with showing just a piece of the cartoon through a small, square window in an envelope. It would be a strong tease, because the recipients can see there is a cartoon inside, but they don't know what it is about. And they won't know until they satisfy their curiosity and open the piece. I think this could have a terrific effect in a campaign, or even as a piece of personal correspondence to an important contact. The other is a new format from R.R. Donnelly, called the "sticky note package." It looks like a standard #10 envelope, but with a yellow sticky note affixed to the outside. They have made it so that the note can be personalized to each recipient, usually in the form of a handwritten note. I am creating a new test package now which will feature the personalized cartoon on the yellow note instead. I expect it will he highly successful.

On-serts: These are single sheets of paper cut to the size of the magazine on which they will ride. They can be affixed with glue or enclosed in a poly bag. As you can see from the examples above, on-serts can be a terrific format for use with a personalized cartoon, and that cartoon can in turn be used to simply draw attention, or even buy down the cost of the campaign, as shown in the *Harvard Business Review* and *Restaurant & Hotel Design* campaigns referenced above.

Freemiums: I'm referencing the Sucrets format above, in which we enclosed a free personalized cartoon print in the actual mailing, rather than holding it back until after the recipient responded to the offer. These are a terrific format for getting a tough audience excited about your offer, and it uses the principle of giving a gift to create favor up front. This is an excellent format to use with cartoons, as suitable-for-framing prints -- and as a low-cost gift that travels well through the mail.

Premiums: Premiums are free gifts given upon receipt of paid orders. These include all sorts of items, from clocks to calculators to radios... wait, all those things are gone now, replaced by apps on smart phones. But cartoons remain just as viable as premiums today as they were years ago. They can be applied to prints, as you have seen from the examples above, but also to coffee mugs, t-shirts, mouse pads and more.

Advantages and disadvantages

Direct marketing, at this point, is at the far end of traditional marketing. There have been efforts to bring it into the digital age, adding pURLs (personalized URLs), scannable barcodes for smart phones and such, but the heyday of direct mail has long since passed. But that can become a big advantage as well. If fewer marketers are using the mail, it stands to reason that those who do will stand out all the more. I believe in the value of contrarian thinking and I think it applies to direct mail now.

There are also some terrific resources available for direct marketers that weren't there in earlier years. Toner-based production allows for some amazing feats in terms of pushing out one-to-one mail pieces in any quantity, overnight. We have a partnership AmazingMail now in which you can order personalized cartoon postcards using a fully automated e-commerce system that allows you to create a campaign in minutes. The amazing thing truly is that the minimum order is one piece, but you can order thousands as well and it all goes in the mail the following day. You can find out more in Chapter 16, where I discuss resources for using cartoons, in this case, in mailings.

The one big disadvantage I see for direct mail is its cost. It has always been expensive compared to other media on a cost per thousand basis, but because it is measurable and precisely targeted, it has often been worth the cost. But with the cost of postage and paper always rising, at some point, it all reaches a tipping point. That point depends on the economics of your particular business, so it varies from company to company and among different industries, but I am concerned that we will see it collapse if that trend continues as it has, unchanged for the past thirty years.

Also counting against direct mail more recently is the green movement, which shuns any use of paper as wasteful. Will this be a temporary trend? We'll only know the answer by staying tuned, but it might be helpful to give a nod to being green in the paper stocks you choose. A recycled stock, along with notice to the audience that you're using these stocks as a way to help preserve the environment would be a positive step toward addressing this possible objection.

Key points to remember

- ✔ Test experience from the use of cartoons in direct marketing is relevant and applicable across all media, platforms and uses

- ✔ The value of that test experience is that it is precisely measured, statistically relevant and proves the effectiveness of cartoons as devices of persuasion

- ✔ Testing has shown when cartoons are focused on recipients' identities, results are maximized

- ✔ Testing has proved that cartoons can be relevant and powerful concerning any subject matter or mission

- ✔ Unlike anything else used in direct marketing, people like to collect personalized cartoons, which boosts response to campaigns

- ✔ People are people, no matter what they do for a living; all are responsive to and appreciate relevant humor

- ✔ Direct mail is one possible application of cartoons as involvement devices, but only one of many

- ✔ Constantly rising postage and paper costs, and concerns about being "green" are two possible disadvantages of direct mail today

- ✔ Cartoons can be used as highly effective premiums in your campaigns, applied to prints, coffee mugs, t-shirts, mouse pads and more

Don't forget to claim your free "Stu Heinecke Dingbats" font
at http://www.CartoonLink.com/claim_font

"I think you must want Johan Strauss the <u>Younger</u>."

Chapter Six

Cartoons in e-mail marketing

Years ago, I took a trip that would change my life. It was my first time ever in Europe and I had several missions in mind. One of those was to meet the girl I'd seen in a magazine, a Danish cover model I was to interview for a film project, who later became my wife. Another was to explore the publishing business in the U.K., including a visit with Michael Ffolkes, whose curlicue cartoon drawings of lusty characters from the late 1800's had fascinated me from his work in *Playboy*.

His studio was a crow's nest located high atop the
Discount Theater Ticket Office, somewhere deep in the heart
of central London. This was one of those impossibly skinny
buildings wedged between two intersecting streets forming
a very narrow angle between them. I recall climbing at least
five stories of spiraling stairs to finally reach his lair, a circular
space decorated in dark wooden paneling with windows all
around and a sprinkling of artwork and odd objects throughout
the room.

I was there to recruit Michael into our group, which
later formed the basis for today's CartoonLink service. I explained how we were injecting personalization into cartoons,
using them as the engine driving people to respond to our
clients' campaigns. I explained the test findings we had already
established, showing that cartoons really were quite powerful
devices for commanding attention and generating truly as-
tounding results.

He seemed to float around the room, as he fixed me
a cup of tea and listened to my pitch. Never sitting still, he
listened intently, speaking on occasion in a quintessential
English gentleman's voice that could have come straight from
any number of movies. It became clear, though, that I was
speaking about things he found quite alien. I was talking about
merging technology with cartooning, while he was busy merging the 1880's with cartooning. It made for an interesting
conversation in which, at one point, he dubbed me, "The man
of the future."

I think he meant it as a compliment. He was also gracious enough to have a look at my own cartoon work, and offered an excellent piece of advice. Back then, my cartooning signature was a mess; my first name stacked above my last in a tangle that left it unreadable. Michael told me, "You'll never become famous if people can't read your signature." It was terrific advice, resulting in the signature I have used ever since. Although I'm still not famous.

Unfortunately, Michael, whose real name was Brian Davis, passed away within a year after we met, so I never had the pleasure of working with him. His inspiring work is a signpost, really, a reminder that there is a cadre of excellent gag cartoonists outside *The New Yorker*, from around the world. Cartooning really is a universal phenomenon, a miracle of humor and truth that is revered throughout most developed cultures. Certainly, there are many outstanding cartoonists from the U.K., including Mike Williams, Roy Raymonde, Ken Mahood, Trevor Holder (Holte) and Terence Parkes (Larry). Much of their work can be found and licensed through the Punch Cartoon Library, which appears in Chapter 16 in this book.

More clicks, opens and response

If Michael Ffolkes found our use of cartoons in direct marketing futuristic, he would have been utterly confounded by their use in e-mail. When we started, I was used to the long lead and response times of mail-based marketing. It typically took six months from the time the creative was submitted, the mailing produced and released, and the response was collected and tallied. In our e-mail campaigns, that process was shortened to minutes, including reading results from competing tests and rolling out the winning package to the rest of the audience.

We accomplished that with a neat trick, a toggling script that allowed us to control which version was seen by the audience. In the first few minutes after launch, the script would distribute each test panel in equal numbers, but as we read the response in real time, the winning test version would reveal itself. And from that point, we set the parameters on the script to present the new "control" to the rest of the recipients. It was utterly amazing to see this process compressed to such a quick and easy task.

For traditional direct marketers, that kind of performance is stunning, although e-mail marketing certainly has evolved into something quite different from direct marketing. Today's e-mail marketing is based on delivering to house lists compiled directly by the marketers, based on strict privacy laws. Delivery has changed from something a marketer does directly from their server to using several excellent, white-listed delivery platforms. These include ConstantContact, iContact, Lyris, and many more. Each has a robust system to ensure that recipients can always opt out, but also includes impressive reporting modules that allow you to watch the performance of your campaign as it unfolds.

If direct marketing was a leap forward for advertising, due to its precise measurement of results and ROI, e-mail is a quantum leap with respect to metrics. Everything is measured. The equivalent in mail marketing would be knowing how many people opened the envelope, who opened the envelope, which elements they touched, who showed it to someone else, what they looked at, and of course, how many people responded to the offer. Some e-mail can go viral, allowing the campaign to reach well beyond the actual delivery list.

Like all forms of marketing, e-mail campaigns require something recipients feel compelled to open, something they can't resist. A lot of marketers resort to newsletters as their solution, but I don't see those creating sustained readership. In fact, their open rates quickly decay after the first issue has been received. Even when the audience is keenly interested in the subject matter, most of us discover we don't have time to read these things. They require too much investment and are mostly self-serving.

Cartoons seem to solve that problem pretty effectively. The audience already knows they're a quick read and that cartoons usually reward the reader with a laugh, perhaps even a new insight. For that reason, we are seeing something extraordinary with cartoons. They seem to generate and sustain unusually high open rates over multiple waves, even in monthly installments over the course of years.

Cartoons have sometimes caused open rates that defy reality. I knew Randy Conrads long ago, just after he founded

Classmates.com. At that point, he had been focused on building the now famous database of high school graduates linked by school and year of graduation, but he had no on-going relationship with these people. I advised that he needed to change that situation, and proposed a Classmates cartoon page, sent weekly to the entire membership base. The page featured a personalized cartoon with a mechanism to forward the cartoon to friends. Weeks later, I asked how it was working, and Randy reported a 130% open rate. Apparently, recipients were either opening the cartoon page more than once or forwarding it to so many friends that the reach exceeded the delivery list by 30%.

That is an extreme case, as are the few 100% response rates we have produced in other campaign types. It's extreme, but it did happen and it confirms the fact that cartoons can play a vital role in your e-mail campaigns.

Uses and formats

While e-mail marketing may be more complex than regular old direct mail, there are really only a few formats to work with. Here are some of the ones that can easily benefit from the inclusion of a cartoon, particularly with personalization and a mechanism to allow recipients to easily forward the piece to friends and colleagues.

Greeting cards: In this format, we have a cleverly-built HTML table which expands where the caption appears in text form. If the user adjusts the type to a larger size, that portion of the card and envelope graphic simply stretch to accommodate the new dimension and all looks natural. I like this format a lot, as it makes the cartoon element look almost like a personal gift. Additional promotional copy, a letter for instance, can be fit just below the card image for a very nice effect.

Flyers: A bit more promotional in tone are flyers, which are clearly sent to get the recipient to respond in some way. These can be used quite effectively as invitations, registration drives for webinars and seminars, sales announcements, couponing and more. The key to a successful campaign seems to be short copy and easily understood links. Obviously, getting recipients to open the piece is always paramount.

Newsletters: If you're already committed to a regular newsletter, it would make sense to include a personalized cartoon featured somewhere in the first page. Use the cartoon as an engagement device and remind readers in your subject line that there is a cartoon about them inside. Use the cartoon to entice recipients to continue to open and read your newsletter. The cartoon will be much more than decoration; it may be the one thing that gets recipients to take notice at all.

Surveys: Using a cartoon at the head of a survey might not make sense at first. Surveys are serious business and the cartoon might influence the answers given. On the other hand, surveys are worthless of no one pays attention to them. Knowing there is a cartoon inside the e-mail becomes a powerful enticement to open it and respond. You could even offer a free print of the cartoon as an incentive for responding.

Discussion forums, blogs: You already know that the nature of a cartoon is to compress issues and topics down to a simple underlying truth. So the addition of a cartoon that gets the audience pointed in the right direction, while enticing them to open the e-mail would make a lot of sense in this mission. Encourage the audience to pass the cartoons along to others and you may have the basis of a viral growth campaign for your forum or blog.

Advantages and disadvantages

There is a lot to like about e-mail marketing. It is precisely measurable in ways we never dreamed about when plying mail-based direct marketing campaigns. The whole process of creating, launching and tabulating a promotion is immediate by comparison, allowing science fiction-like possibilities of testing during the first fifteen minutes of response, then rolling out the winning test panel as your new "control." E-mail marketing has come a long way in the past five years, with the launch of white-listed delivery platforms, which make list hygiene and campaigning turnkey and provide robust reporting to steer the way. My favorite benefit is that e-mail marketing is inexpensive -- dirt cheap, really -- in comparison to all other media platforms, making it easier to foster more active relationships with your client and prospect base and to generate sufficient ROI on your marketing spend.

The big disadvantage plaguing e-mail marketing is spam. There are sinister users of e-mail, and their mostly offensive e-mails arrive right next to yours in recipients' in-boxes. Spamming is illegal and there are stiff penalties in place to curb the practice. Unfortunately, some e-mail users are all too anxious to lodge well-placed complaints that can hurt your business, regardless of whether the complaint is justified or not. However, by using the delivery services mentioned here, that problem is all but eliminated, as long as you're starting with a clean list of opted-in customers and prospects, which is easy enough to do.

I think the final advantage of e-mail is that it works quite well with cartoons, and cartoons work quite well in return, pushing open rates way up and keeping them there over extended periods of time. So, which is best for e-mail, personalized or non-personalized cartoons? If the list includes first and last name data, I recommend using personalization. It causes recipients to be more curious, because they want to know what new cartoon you've sent about themselves. It's a powerful draw. If name data is not available, I would urge finding a way to append it to your files. It's worth the investment. But if it just isn't possible to do, then proceed with a non-personalized cartoon that amplifies your point. That will also be worth the investment, making your e-mail compelling reading every time it chimes its arrival in recipients' in-boxes.

Key points to remember

- ✔ E-mail is a tremendous platform for promotions, due to its immediacy, metrics and extremely low cost

- ✔ Cartoons are powerful devices for attracting high open and read rates, sustained over multiple touches and long campaign durations

- ✔ E-mail is easier than ever to launch and manage, thanks to white-listed delivery platforms such as ConstantContact, iContact and more

- ✔ E-mail makes it possible to compress the test/roll-out cycle to minutes

- ✔ Whenever possible, use personalized cartoons in your promotions to spur more involvement with your e-mails

Don't forget to claim your free "Stu Heinecke Dingbats" font
at http://www.CartoonLink.com/claim_font

"Today, what little remained of all the money in the world disappeared into the pockets of David Friedman and three or four lawyers from New Jersey."

Chapter Seven

Cartoons in print advertising

I've only met Jack Ziegler once, but it was a thrill, as he is also one of my heros of cartooning. It was in the cartoonists' waiting room on the 14th floor in *The New Yorker's* old building on 45th Street, a drab off-white room sparsely appointed with a few chairs and a couch. This was one of those visits to the cartooning floor on review day, when many of the greats congregated to show the editor their weekly output of cartoon roughs, in hopes of making a sale. I have never relied on such an obstacle course to make my living, so I don't know quite what it must be like to sit there, wondering if you'll earn something from your past week's work.

It must be wearing, because every one of the cartoonists in the lobby looked nervous, almost defeated. I have always found that so odd, because these are some of the world's best cartoonists who have appeared in the magazine regularly. But the day's stress didn't show on Jack Ziegler's face. And I suppose he had good reason. His work is consistently brilliant and his output of ideas is prodigious. I read once that Jack has file cabinets filled with unpublished roughs, something on the order of 12,000 cartoons in waiting.

I have two favorite cartoons by Jack, but these are merely two I remember easily. His work is so funny and his images so well drawn in his literal yet cartoonish style that they're all worthy of admiration. These favorites are both sight gags; the first depicts a first-time boat owner leaning way over the transom of his new sport fisherman yacht, holding a bucket of black paint as he applies it's new name, *"My First Boat,"* which is painted upside down. The other shows a very typical New York deli restaurant with a script-style sign mounted across the width of the establishment that reads, *"Eat 'n Pay 'n Get Out."*

Other than his astonishing output of spectacular cartoons, I have to admit I don't know a lot about Jack, except that he moves around the country a lot. That might explain it right there. Since I first met him, Jack has lived in New York, then Connecticut, then Las Vegas, then back to Connecticut and now he's somewhere in the Mid-West, I believe. I may have missed a few moves in between as well. But that doesn't matter, because you can easily locate plenty of Jack's work in the Cartoon Bank archive. If you choose anything by him for your projects and campaigns, you're getting one of the very best cartoonists in the world on your team.

Pivotal campaigns

I need to start by acknowledging the power of branding. Brands have enormous influence in our lives, as they form the basis for most of the purchasing decisions we make. I have used Apple products my entire career, I once owned a Ferrari and I mostly feel that if I don't buy name-brand items, I'm cheating myself out of receiving the best quality goods and services. I actually have to fight those thoughts to make more rational, if not completely satisfying, decisions on which car to drive, which can of peas to buy and so on. The effect of brand advertising is enormous and it all stems from mass media exposure, including print.

Still, I must admit to having an uneasy relationship with print advertising as it relates to the use of cartoons -- or anything else. I would like to provide examples of test-proven, pivotal print campaigns that have involved cartoons, but that just is not the nature of the medium. Full-page ads in magazines and newspapers are impressive, which is why they're so useful for branding, but it is nearly impossible to get a solid measurement on any effect they might have.

My professional growth occurred within the bounds of direct marketing, I grew up on the belief that everything you do in marketing should be measurable or it's not worthwhile. But how to do you measure the effect of branding? Ad agencies do their best, conducting surveys, counting coupon responses, quizzing focus groups, but it could have just as easily been the fact that it rained the week your campaign for the raincoat client ran that caused sales to jump. There just is no way to know for sure what effect most print ads have on the advertisers' sales, which leave us with no results to point to concerning the use of cartoons.

That doesn't stop us from applying a bit of logic, though. Readership surveys have already told us cartoons are almost always the best read and remembered part of magazines and newspapers, so it makes sense to put that effect to work in ads appearing in those same magazines and newspapers. We're just going to have to judge based on slightly different criteria, because the metrics just aren't there.

Having worked with magazines as my core clientele all these years, I have an insider's perspective on what I see as a continued downfall. The dot-com meltdown took a lot of their ad revenue away and it never returned to its original level. Instead, the shock of 9/11 kept ad budgets depressed for a while and when ad spending came back, most of it diverted to digital media, where metrics are king. Still, you can't perfume a Web page and 468-by-60 pixels worth of banner real estate doesn't come close to the impact of a full page in a magazine or newspaper. I think there will continue to be a paper-based publishing industry, but it has not come close to its equilibrium point. Much of what print was will start showing up on the mobile tablet platform, though, which will be spectacular in effect and function, and "print" will finally participate in the metrics revolution.

So let's suspend belief for a brief time, let's imagine advertising in a world where measurement, results and ROI are irrelevant, where all that matters is the compelling nature of the concept.

Uses and formats

From earlier chapters you know that cartoons used for campaigns are viewed in terms of their underlying truth. Any print strategy concerning the use of a cartoon should be directed based on the point of agreement carried forward by the truth revealed in the gag. It should not be made self-serving, by injecting your or your client's brand. That would be a costly mistake, because the ad won't produce the desired results. In fact, it will be counterproductive, leaving you further from your goal, due to the negative impression that would leave with readers. Steer by the underlying truth only, make sure it establishes a point of agreement you can build on with the audience. The best scenario will likely be illustrating a point about the need your service or product serves -- without mentioning your product or service or brand in the cartoon.

Beyond that, it is important to remember what we have here. A nugget of truth that creates agreement among the audience that your service or product truly is needed. And something that dominates the readership and memorability readings in print. It's something readers can't ignore, which is a very powerful position to start from. With that, here are three possible creative strategies; these are what I would do if my assignment was to create a new print campaign for a client.

Editorial look: You've seen the special supplements in magazines, the throw-away sections that suddenly show up while you page through the magazine and just don't look or feel quite right. The paper is heavier, glossier. The type and lay-out just don't quite mesh with the rest of the publication. Those are "advertorials," and magazines do their best to make sure those don't blend in with the rest of the magazine. It's for a good reason; magazines have a reputation to maintain with their readers as objective reporters of the truth. They often refer to that discipline as, "the separation of church and state," the ironclad notion that there is no possibility that advertisers can unduly influence editorial coverage.

I think cartoons offer a way around that. In *The New Yorker*, for example, there are ads that devote most of their space to a cartoon done by one of the regular cartoonists. That's smart, because we already know that readers actually do peruse the cartoons first, before they read anything else in the magazine. So the ad is going to get noticed, whether or not it is labeled, "Paid Advertisement" at the top of the space. It's going to get read, but here's what's not smart. I surveyed several of these ads in the magazine in preparation for this book, and I can tell you that every one of them featured a cartoon about the brand. Big mistake, terrible strategic thinking. But you know better, because you know how to properly steer a cartoon for your campaign, based on the underlying truth, not on blindly pushing your brand into the cartoon and killing all possibility of making it funny or appreciated by readers. If there is no humor or if the humor is self-serving, you will defeat the effectiveness of your campaign.

Cartoon as a counterpoint: Earlier in this book, I talked about the need to place cartoons in context, and I mentioned a newspaper ad I really admired. If you will recall, it featured a cartoon depicting the truth about the need to constantly update computer equipment. The ad was placed on behalf of Digital Equipment Company, as part of their effort to launch an advanced new line of computers that was supposed to provide a much longer lifecycle. So while the cartoon revealed the truth about the need to replace computers almost annually, the designers of the ad included a brilliant layer of context. The ad showed the cartoon on a piece of newsprint, as though it had been torn out of a newspaper and thumbtacked to a bulletin board. That created separation from the rest of the ad and its message, which was headlined with the words, "Get Serious." They created a very effective job of positioning the two as opposing counterpoints. I like this approach a lot, and can imagine using a number of visual devices to create that separation. So in this creative strategy, you're first choosing a cartoon that makes the opposite point to the one you want to make, isolating it graphically, then making your counterpoint in the headline and copy.

Just the cartoon alone: It's a gutsy strategy, but I can picture it being very powerful and effective. How about letting the cartoon do all of your talking, by featuring just the cartoon with your identity and contact information below? If we have full confidence the cartoon makes the right point, why dilute the message with more copy? I don't mean to be overly repetitive, but it needs to be said: if you're going to follow this creative strategy, make sure you follow my rules! Don't focus on your identity in the cartoon, focus on the truth. Free of unnecessary constraints, the cartoon will do the rest for you in a most elegant way.

Personalization versus no personalization: Throughout the book, I have included discussion about whether to use personalization in the cartoon or not. It seems pointless to bring it up here, because we are talking about print advertising, after all. Well it turns out personalization is available, through a process called selective binding. I want you to know that I do not recommend spending the money. Print is a blunt instrument; we just need to see it for what it is. But if the idea of personalization in full page, full color ads makes sense to you, you're going to love advertising in magazines on the mobile tablet platform. That promises to be stunning in every possible way, from the graphics, functionality, metrics, connectivity and frictionless transactions and commerce, making use of personalization will be a simple matter, and I believe it will also be an effective new use of personalization and cartoons. You can read about cartoons in mobile advertising in the next chapter.

Advantages and disadvantages

There is still one big advantage to print advertising, and that is impact. A full page ad in a magazine or newspaper is impressive. It provides the reader with great vistas in which to soak up your branding message. Magazines and newspapers are also the venue in which cartoons have proved to be so well read and remembered in readership surveys. So it makes sense to think about using a cartoon to draw attention to your advertising message.

As with all other media, if you choose the right cartoon based on its underlying truth, and align your advertising message with it, this can have a powerful effect. I think cartoons in print should match their setting, so in a newspaper ad, it might make sense to use a syndicated feature to draw attention. In magazines, use the single-panel *New Yorker* style cartoon I have been writing about in this book, to make your ad fit with the editorial setting. Either way, these will draw attention.

But we're talking about the great dinosaur of the advertising world. To many marketers, advertising means metrics, results and ROI, and print simply cannot keep pace. But have you thought of placing a full-page ad in a tablet magazine or newspaper? It will have everything you like, plus metrics and functionality print advertising could never match. If that piques your curiosity, be sure to read the next chapter, "Cartoons in mobile advertising."

Key points to remember

- ✓ Because print is essentially unmeasurable, no one really knows what effect print ads have with precise certainty

- ✓ Cartoons can still be extremely effective tools in print ads, based on readership survey findings

- ✓ There are several creative strategies you can use to take advantage of the power of cartoons in print advertising

- ✓ Personalization is possible, but not recommended in print advertising

- ✓ If you like print ads, start looking to publications on the mobile tablet platform for amazing new advertising opportunities

Don't forget to claim your free "Stu Heinecke Dingbats" font
at http://www.CartoonLink.com/claim_font

"OK. Heads we take a tiny pay-cut, tails, we fire a bunch of people."

Chapter Eight

Cartoons in mobile advertising

Mick Stevens is a master at cartooning. The characters who inhabit his drawings somehow make me think of doodles drawn by a badly misbehaving kid; there's just a mischievous quality to his cartoons that is hard to describe. Masters of any art know how to project elements of a story through mere suggestion, with the minimal amount of lines, shading and detail. When you take in one of Mick's cartoons, sensory details hit your brain that couldn't possibly be in the actual drawing; you can hear the background noise, you can pick up smells in the room, you're fully transported for that brief moment into the scene Mick has portrayed for you.

As a cartoonist myself, I have admired Mick's work for a long time. I marvel at how he makes his drawings work so well, how it seems as though he has subtracted lines to make his characters more sparse, yet more expressive. If you take a close look, you'll see that the faces of the characters aren't completely drawn. The line that should define an entire side of the face isn't even there, it's just suggested. Just the thought of some of the characters I've seen in his cartoons bring a smile to my face. They're funny without having said a word. It's brilliant stuff.

Cartooning appears to be simply a discipline of drawing, but writing is actually its core. There are no finer examples of great gag construction than in Mick's work. It's with good reason that he has been a regular contributing cartoonist to *The New Yorker* since the 1970s.

I have only known Mick personally for a very short time. But already, I can see he is an adventurous soul, someone who likes to live life fully, someone who likes to explore new uses of cartoons. He was a collaborator with Matt Diffee on the *Rejection Collection* book series and part of an effort now to launch a new cartoon magazine on the tablet platform. Having had the opportunity to get to know him over the past several months, I can see that he will be a joy to collaborate with on the magazine project and so many others.

Mick's work is available for use in your projects and campaigns as well, through the Cartoon Bank, perhaps later in my own CartoonLink programs. As with all of the cartoonists introduced in this book, I highly recommend his brilliant work.

The promise of the iPad and other tablets

Thinking about the promise of the mobile tablet platform, I can barely contain my enthusiasm and awe. Apple only admitted to the existence of the iPad in January 2010. The product launched in March and by the end of that year, the company had already sold 13.5 million units. They are projected to sell another 45 million units in 2011, while competing tablets find their way to market, accounting for as many as 80 million units in consumers hands by the end of the year. That is an explosion, a sudden deployment of a new platform anchored by a new class of device that people happily fill with paid content. The opportunity to publish new magazines, deploy new forms of advertising, make new fortunes selling countless apps is historic and stunning. If you thought the rise of the Internet was impressive, you will be astonished by what is about to unfold on the mobile tablet platform.

If you are an advertiser, your palette has been expanding for some time, starting with the mobile advertising and app revolution bought by smart phones. At this writing, there are currently more than 300,000 app in the Apple App Store, with a smaller number on competing stores. They do everything imaginable, turning iPhones, iPads and iPods into the most versatile devices in the history of mankind. They can listen to a song and identify it, tell you if your flight is on time, turn your phone into a level, compass or barcode scanner and allow you to play thousands of games including my favorite, *Labyrinth*, the game of tilting a wooden maze to guide a marble through without falling into a hole. Many of these functionalities are easily converted to compelling ads.

Imagine an ad, for example, that is a Labyrinth board, which allows you to play the game until you guide the marble all the way through the maze to earn a $25 gift card at Target. Wouldn't an ad for Stanley Tools be smashing if it turned your tablet into a level or wall stud finder? If you were a handyman, you'd return to the ad constantly, just for the chance to use the tools within. How about an ad that includes a real-time map showing where you are and where the nearest Quizno's shops are and has a constantly updated set of coupons you can use to save on lunch?

The age of ads as apps and apps as ads is already here and it's about to get much bigger as the tablet platform explodes. If you're not familiar with the mobile ad space, HTML5 and the workings of the new tablets, you need to get there fast.

Truly stunning functionality

So far, print has been the medium for ads that create big branding impact. Nothing in the digital realm can compete with the aesthetic of a full page, full color ad in a magazine, or the physical impact of a full page ad in a newspaper. That is about to come to an abrupt end, with the emergence of full-page ads on tablets.

Sure, the size of the tablet screen still doesn't compare with that of a full page in a newspaper, but who wants to lug around something that big any way? Just watch someone trying to read a newspaper on a crowded subway and you'll see how silly it has become to read newsprint on something three-and-half-feet wide and two feet tall.

But the impact a full-page ad will have on a tablet will go far beyond anything we have yet seen. The functionality of things in our lives is growing exponentially. And it all stems from the spectrum of things apps do for our lives. As advertisers, we need to think in terms of our ads being stand-alone apps, something our target audience will find useful and want to keep and use. That's going to be a lot of fun for everyone involved.

Based on what we've seen with smart phones and iPads, we know that there are certain functionalities already on hand for our use. Accelerometers allow tablets to sense motion and tilt, an essential for many gaming-based apps and ads. GPS and real time mapping allow users to pinpoint their location in relation to where you want to drive them through your ads. Apple left it out of the first version, but there is no question iPads will have to incorporate telephony and FaceTime. Imagine the connection you'll be able to establish with customers when they can video conference with customer service reps within your tablet ads.

Tablets, along with smart phones, iPods and e-readers are a new class of device that people gladly fill with paid content. And the same mechanism that allows one-touch purchases of music and apps can be applied to your ads as well, opening the door to a new platform for frictionless transactions. Imagine readers flipping through a tablet magazine, finding an ad for a chair they particularly like, and tapping a button once to make the purchase, even though they have no direct account with the advertiser. It's coming to an iPad near you and as an advertiser, you should be looking for ways to use this platform.

Where do cartoons fit in?

In the previous chapter, I discussed the approaches I thought would work best in print ads, but I also expressed my lack of enthusiasm for the print medium. Those shortcomings disappear when translated to the mobile and particularly tablet space. Full page ads within a tablet magazine will be just as stunning as those found in high-end magazines, but with the digital metrics advertisers now demand. The portability, the personal relationship we'll have with our tablet devices and the stunning functionality they afford will transform the art of using full page ads to brand, sell and engage the audience will make this the ultimate advertising platform.

How do I know this? I have been studying the emergence of the e-paper platform for the past ten to fifteen years. That's how long magazine and newspaper publishers have been discussing the new future of their medium, while electronics giants have been plying their gee-whiz prototypes at the Consumer Electronics Show every January in Las Vegas. Phillips has been showing thin-film, touch-screen monitors you simply roll up and throw in your backpack when you're finished reading. Fast forward to today, I am in the midst of starting a new incubator venture that will launch new magazines onto the tablet platform. I'm intimately involved in where this is going, and I can tell you it is truly astonishing.

As we plan our new magazine concepts, personalized cartoons have already found their way in. I expect they will become part of the editorial product, because we'll have the ability to easily insert data from a subscriber's account. So in a cooking magazine, you're likely to see cartoons about your cooking; in a pet magazine your dog or cat might be featured as little surprises throughout.

If a personalized cartoon makes sense editorially, then why not as the draw for an ad? The same rules defined in Chapter 4 apply to all of the missions described in this book, so you'll need to steer the message based on the underlying truth of the cartoon. The same ad types described in the earlier chapter on print advertising would still apply, so you'd want to make the cartoon look like it is part of the editorial content as much as possible. Or you could present the cartoon as a counter to your point, using graphic separation to lead the reader in your direction. The big difference is that you will have the option of personalization in your cartoon, which I would highly recommend.

Keep in mind that ads in the mobile space should strive to reach the status of a prized app that the reader will return to constantly. Perhaps your cartoon ad could be a daily series of cartoons, something the reader can check every day to see the new installment. Make it easy for the reader to save your ad to their home screen as an app icon. Make it easy to use continually, perhaps in the form of a daily calendar or appointment diary. I think you can already imagine how a daily cartoon element will make your ad highly compelling to readers.

No one can say for sure what the mobile platform will evolve into. Who knows what tablets will be capable of doing in ten years? Whatever that is, I am sure cartoons will continue to be supremely powerful devices to attract attention throughout that evolutionary path.

And what about smart phones? They're part of the mobile platform and there are billion mobile phones in consumers' hands now, but the small screens are a significant limiting factor. There may be terrific applications for cartoons on cell phones, but I haven't seen anything that looks very exciting.

Maybe it's just those small screens, which is why my focus remains squarely on the tablet portion of the mobile market.

Advantages and disadvantages

This is an exploding opportunity for advertisers, publishers and app developers. It's a stunning, historic opportunity to create new fortunes, new ways of doing business. If you are employed in the advertising business, this is where you need to go to find your next big push in your career. If you are an advertiser, particularly a print user, you must find your way onto this platform. It will give you everything you like about print, plus so much more. I predict these will be some of the most effective forms of advertising ever devised.

Certainly, cartoons can provide the advantages they have always brought to other forms of advertising; they'll still be some of the most read and remembered part of magazines, newspapers and other forms of content delivery on the tablet platform. The ads may look just like they do now in print, but you'll have the option of personalizing the cartoons in your ads, which will be a terrific tool for drawing attention and generating results.

This may be the opportunity of a lifetime for many of us, one of the biggest shifts in the delivery of content, entertainment and advertising we may ever see. So are there any disadvantages? It's too soon to tell. The biggest disadvantage I can see is simply the lack of available programmers to help us create the ads.

Key points to remember

- ✓ The tablet platform is exploding, with a projected 80 million units in consumers' hands by the end of 2011

- ✓ The mobile tablet platform represents one of the most stunning opportunities of our lifetime for advertisers

- ✓ Ads can be re-imagined as apps, using far more functionality to capture an audience's attention constantly

- ✓ Tablet ads can be programmed to continually update with new content, as in a calendar that reveals a new cartoon each day

- ✓ Ads can be set up to be easy for readers to save as icons on home screens for repeated viewing and use

- ✓ Cartoons can play a significant role as attention and engagement devices for mobile ads

© Matt Diffee

The Vesparados

DIFFE

Chapter Nine

Cartoons in VIP contact campaigns

I have introduced you to many of my heroes of cartooning in preceding chapters, cartoonists whom I have admired for a long time, and for the most part, people who are somewhat older than I am. Matt Diffee doesn't fit into that box or any other, for that matter. He breaks the mold in so many ways

and represents the new guard among the cast of cartoonists in
The New Yorker.

It took me a while to warm up to Matt's work, which
first started appearing in the magazine in 1999. His drawing
style is wholly different from the sparse, free-form pen and
ink drawings of his predecessors. Matt's drawings are studied,
realistic pencil sketches that come across almost as black and
white photographs, the effect completed by a squared, straight-
line frame around the perimeter. Yet, for all their trained-artist
discipline, there is an always noticeable undertow of playful-
ness. Two favorites immediately come to mind. The first is
a sight gag showing Che Guevarra in that famous pose from
revolutionary posters and later, t-shirts, himself wearing a
t-shirt bearing the image of Bart Simpson. The other is of a
sleazy character slumped in a fold-out chair, taking a drag on
his cigarette as he holds a paint roller in his other hand. It's obvious he is a sidewalk vendor from the sign at his side, which
says, *"Face Painting, $5."* That would be the worst five bucks
you'd ever waste on the streets of New York.

Matt breaks the mold in so many other ways as well.
Most cartoonists would describe themselves as shy, Matt is a
stand-up comedian when he's not drawing. For most cartoonists, it takes a long time to rise to the level of breaking into
The New Yorker, Matt did it at a young age after entering a contest.
And most cartoonists tend to leave the affairs of business to
others, but Matt is a natural leader and a vocal advocate for
the art form.

In 2006, he had a masterstroke, a lot like Bob Mankoff's original idea that resulted in the formation of the Cartoon Bank. Realizing that most of the work submitted to *The New Yorker* was being rejected, Matt approached his fellow cartoonists with a brilliant idea: Let's do a book. And so was born *The Rejection Collection*, followed by a second edition, *The Rejection Collection Vol. 2: The Cream of the Crap*. Watch for great things from Matt in the future, too. I expect he will be the next cartoon editor for *The New Yorker* when Bob Mankoff retires.

I've only known Matt for a short while as well, but look forward to his collaboration with a new cartooning magazine on the tablet platform, along with Mick Stevens. It will be exciting to see where that goes. In the meantime, you can confidently choose Matt as a collaborator in your projects by using his cartoons in your projects and campaigns. To do that, you can license his work from the Cartoon Bank, or visit matthewdiffee.com. You can also see Matt live on steampoweredhour.com.

What are contact campaigns?

From the very beginning of my use of cartoons in direct marketing, I discovered they were also very effective as devices to get ahold of people I needed to reach. Contact campaigning became my own personal secret weapon, because the more

I played with it, the more I found that I could reach virtually anyone. And I do mean anyone.

I once sent a framed cartoon to President Bush (senior), showing a guy practice-putting in his office while his assistant pokes her head in the door asking, *"Would you mind if President Bush plays through?"* He wrote a personal note back, telling me about how his golf game had been suffering recently and that he probably should practice more. I'm pretty sure that wasn't a form letter. That is how I have reached out to several Presidents, the Prime Minister of Canada, various celebrities, countless CEOs and even more top decision makers who were critical to my success in business.

For nearly thirty years, I kept most of this to myself, happily reaching people I otherwise would have had no business contacting. It was like a free pass to wherever I wanted to go, to meet anyone I wanted, and most importantly, stitch together deals that have helped grow my business. Then I started putting it to work for clients here and there.

At one point, I was working on a new program for my client, *The Wall Street Journal*, which required partnerships with large point-based reward programs. So I sought out one of the biggest, American Express Membership Rewards. I knew I couldn't just call the switchboard and ask for the person in charge of partnerships for their points program, so instead, I used one of my contact campaigns to reach out their CEO, Ken Chenault. This time, I sent a suitable for framing print of a cartoon showing cows grazing in a field, with a title across the top that said, *"Bad Cow Disease."* One of the cows is saying to another, *"Pssst, I know where Ken Chenault keeps his credit cards. Pass it on..."*

With the print I included a letter telling Mr. Chenault what I wanted to accomplish, with a request for a referral to the right person at the company. I followed up the next day with one of what must have been ten assistants, asking if my letter had been received. She was about to dismiss me with a, "if he's interested, we'll call you..." But I broke in and told her if they did receive my letter, they would remember it because it came with a cartoon print about Mr. Chenault. "Oh, you're the one who sent that! Hold on..." was her response, and thirty seconds later I had my referral from the CEO's office. Needless to say, the deal did get done.

Contact campaigning has become my favorite form of promotion. I've been curious all these years if anyone has been doing anything similar, but there just isn't a lot of information out there. At one point, I wrote an article for Manta.com, citing ten methods for reaching VIP contacts. My research turned up some interesting alternative forms of contact campaigning. The most fascinating of those involved running a full-page newspaper ad in *The Wall Street Journal*, targeted to one person. This was used once when someone wanted to reach Larry Ellison, the notoriously difficult to reach CEO of Oracle. Because of the widespread readership of the paper, the target contact has people streaming in all day, asking if he'd seen the ad in that day's paper. The problem is, this can easily cost ten thousand dollars to do, and for most people, that's just too much to risk to take for a single contact.

But that brings up an important point about contact campaigning -- the numbers are quite bizarre. If you're used to using direct mail, for instance, you want to get your cost down to well below a dollar per piece including postage. In contact campaigning, we're talking about aiming something on the order of a framed print at a single target contact, so the cost per piece can easily settle in at a few hundred dollars. That may sound excessive until you consider the upside. If, by sending a $200 contact campaign piece, you end up selling a fifty thousand dollar contract, that is an enormous profit and return on investment. When have you ever heard of a campaign producing a 25,000% ROI? In fact, some of our clients are seeing even better returns.

You may have noticed that one of the forewords to this book was written by Bruce Seidman, President of Sandler Training. Sandler Training is an amazing company, founded by David Sandler, who discovered an entirely new and far more effective way of selling. They have over 250 franchised offices all over the world, serving a client base of more than one hundred thousand clients. I knew I had to set up a partnership with them somehow, so that they would become resellers of our contact campaign system called CartoonLink BigBoards™ (I'm holding an example on the cover of the book). So I sent one to Mr. Seidman, which resulted in a terrific new relationship and a budding new partnership in the coming year. Best practice dictates that you test before you roll out, and that was the case with Sandler, starting with a small series of tests by a few hand-picked franchisees. The first test consisted of our CartoonLink BigBoards™ being sent to five *Fortune* 1000 CEOs; all five called the Sandler franchisee and agreed to meet, and two signed up on the spot for training programs. My math may be off, and I can't reveal actual figures, but it looks like that test produced a 100,000% ROI -- and yet another 100% response rate.

Nearly every big result in my career, every good thing that has happened to me, has come as a result of using contact campaigns. If you visit USPS.com, you can buy CartoonLink cards through their PremiumPostcard program. That deal was set up as a result of sending a set of three framed, personalized cartoon postcards to the manager in charge of the program. Every one of the record-breaking campaigns I created for many of the world's biggest direct marketers, including *Ad Age, Forbes, Harvard Business Review, Time Inc., The Wall Street Journal,* AT&T, the NBA and NHL league offices and many more, all came as a result of my first sending some form of contact campaign featuring a personalized cartoon.

I mentioned that I have experimented with a number of formats. Framed prints with an accompanying letter have worked well, but these require special packaging to prevent breakage, which requires custom-manufactured pieces you have to buy in quantity and warehouse, all of which makes this alternative too bulky and expensive. Suitable for framing prints are just large pieces of paper, so they ship easily, and have proven effective, but again, they require custom packaging which requires an up-front investment and unwieldy warehousing requirements. The format I favor is what we have based our CartoonLink BigBoards Program on. These are nearly two by three foot pieces produced on quarter-inch foam board, with a personalized cartoon on the front and a personal message from the sender to the target recipient on the back. I have found that the best way to produce and deliver these is by using a sign shop closest to the end destination. The foam board is actually a common form of digitally-produced indoor signage, so most sign shops readily handle the job. From there, we hire a local courier to deliver the piece to the target contact's lobby.

This is a constant learning process, so I'm always discovering more about how contact campaigning works and new tricks to make it even more effective. That often comes from clients using our BigBoards system. In the Sandler Training test above, one of the franchisees found that it helped to have their BigBoards delivered by someone who has actually had training in the Sandler system. He feels that a courier only has the ability to drop off the board, whereas a trained operative has the ability to sit down with the CEO right away and talk about what they offer if it comes up. Some clients don't just want to use the BigBoards to reach new prospects, they want to use them to thank their best clients. We have designed a version of the BigBoards that includes an annual calendar next to the cartoon, to ensure that the piece remains on display and in use for at least a year. It makes sense, because your best clients are just as capable as any prospect of awarding you a lucrative new contract.

Sales promotion versus strategic business development

It seems there is a lot of confusion regarding the difference between sales and business development. I hear people using the
terms interchangeably, which is wrong. It's important to see
the two clearly, side by side, because they each define distinctly
different missions which are important to any enterprise. Sales
is the direct interaction with clients and prospects for the purpose of generating transactions involving payment for goods or
services. Business development is the pursuit of strategic partnerships, positions or market advantages that result in greater
scale and often some form of revenue split between the parties. Sales is the process of exchanging goods and services for
money; business development is the process that takes place
before sales occur, to open vast new channels for sales figures
to grow. If the party is handing you a check for whatever it is
your company offers, it's sales. If no money changes hands in
the course of securing a deal between you and the other party,
it's business development.

Every company needs to sell to survive. Not every
company seems to have caught on to the benefits of strategic
business development, which can be an incredibly effective
shortcut to rapidly increase sales. When I approached the US
Postal Service, I wasn't looking to sell them anything. Instead,
I was looking for a partnership, an agreement to start selling
CartoonLink postcards on USPS.com, through their PremiumPostcard program. They have a far bigger sales channel
than I could ever create on my own, so it makes perfect sense
to find a way to be a part of it. I'm a big believer in the use of

business development as a growth strategy, and every step of the way, I have found contact campaigning to be an invaluable tool for making that happen.

Whether you're directly selling or seeking business development deals, you need to figure out who to target. Tony Parinello, author of *Selling to VITO* (Very Important Top Officer), says selling to the CEO, president or owner is the only way to go. I agree with him completely.

Selling at the top means you're talking to the end decision maker, someone who isn't constrained by budgets, someone who can make a decision on the spot. Selling at the top also means bigger sales, because that is where the big decisions are made.

But first you have to make contact, which is never easy. If you're finding yourself shut out of the executive suite, you haven't been singled out. It's hard to reach VIPs because they are important and because they are very busy. They constantly have to make tough choices about how they will invest that time and with whom. If you're not someone they know, you have only the slimmest chance of getting through.

With your newfound power comes great responsibility

Using contact campaigns gives you new power to access virtually anyone, but it comes with a new level of responsibility. CEOs can reach one another easily, in part because they understand how valuable their counterparts' time is. They know how to make immediate and effective use of their time together, and how to organize their thoughts before calling the meeting. As a user of contact campaigns in your business, you need to rise to that same level. The worst thing you can do is pique a CEO's interest enough to score a meeting, then waste his or her time.

Before you request a meeting, check your thinking, make sure you know what the target's business is, where their areas of pain are and how you can help. Know the CEOs personal history, check for news and press releases, understand their situation before you set up the call. This doesn't require a lot of time, either. If you use Google, Manta and Hoover's, as well as a quick sweep of the target contact's site, you can get a pretty quick and useful snapshot of your target before releasing the contact campaign to get in touch.

BigBoards and other contact campaign regimes can get you in the door, but what is your plan once you're there? Obviously, you need to have your thoughts organized into a concise agenda, but you've also got to approach the meeting with a great deal of flexibility. Don't worry if you didn't get to finish your presentation, you can finish expressing your thoughts later with an e-mail or a second meeting. The thing you should strive for is a sense of confidence on the part of your new contact that they can count on you for clear thinking and real solutions. To get there, you'll have to do a lot more listening than talking and shape your solutions to their needs.

This brief section is not meant to teach you how to make the most of your meetings with VIP contacts, it's simply to explain that you can get in the door using cartoons as your secret weapon. For further reading on how to conduct effective meetings with CEOs and other VIPs, I recommend another book called *Five Minutes with VITO*, co-authored by Tony Parinello and Sandler Training CEO David Mattson.

Executive assistants and top-down referrals

Executive assistants play an important role in their employer's affairs that is greatly underestimated. These are highly intelligent people who are firmly in charge of whether you get through or not, and whether your deal happens or not. No access, no deal. So they need to be recognized for what they are: your potential allies.

When I'm pursuing a deal with an important prospective partner, I welcome my chance to speak with assistants and I think they sense it. I treat them as equals, I explain who I am, what I want to accomplish and seek their guidance as to how to break through. I extend my trust to them, and most times, I am rewarded with their expert assistance. If I have used a cartoon piece to open the contact, I often follow up with a card to the assistant to offer thanks, but also to reward them for letting me through.

There are also times when an assistant may offer a referral to someone else in the organization. These can either be an enabling bit of guidance or a brush-off, so I'm always careful to ask questions to understand the basis of the referral. These have often been right on target and have helped me get the deal done, but even when they don't produce the desired results, I maintain a positive relationship with the executive assistant, as I may need to come back for more direction.

Advantages and disadvantages

VIP contact campaigning allows us access to people who can change the fortunes of our companies and open potentially huge new sales channels we would never be able to create ourselves. Even when I'm using BigBoards to generate a single point of sale, I know that by targeting the right kinds of prospects, I can produce great gains for myself and my company. I find it just as exciting to help my clients produce those gains for their enterprises. Contact campaigning is in some ways like direct mail on steroids. The campaign pieces are not simple #10 business envelopes with a letter, they're framed prints or giant foam core postcards with bizarre levels of production value and equally bizarre levels of success, where ROI figures can reach into the tens of thousands or higher. No other form of promotion comes close to producing a 100,000% return on investment. And that's exciting.

Contact campaigns can be used for many missions, from prospecting the CEO of a big company for a big sale, to thanking your best clients for their valued business, to just about anything else you could imagine. I'm about to launch new contact campaigns to several U.S. Senators to suggest a bill, while another will go to the executive vice president of a *Fortune* 500 company to strike up a multi-level deal worth potentially millions of dollars to my company. You can be doing the same thing, too. The sky truly is the limit.

But if you decide to participate in contact campaigning, you'll need to be smart about it. Having the power to contact VIPs requires that you take great care in being prepared for resulting meetings. It's hard to explain the financials of contact campaigning without sounding irrational. The contact pieces are expensive, but the campaigns are small in number, so their overall expense is low. When a contact campaign connects, resulting in big contracts or new access to new sales channels, the value can be astronomical.

There are potential disadvantages. If you don't target your contact campaign audience carefully, you may miss the big profit potential. If you reach a VIP and are unprepared to follow through with a productive meeting, then contact campaigns will be an expensive waste of your time and theirs.

Key points to remember

- ✔ Contact campaigning is the process of breaking through to unreachable VIPs, CEOs and key decision-makers who have the potential to change the scale of your business

- ✔ VIPs are unreachable because they're busy and their time is valuable

- ✔ Contact campaigning can be used to cultivate sales, thank a prime customer, strike up a partnership or virtually any other purpose you can imagine

- ✔ Welcome the opportunity to work with executive assistants; treat them as allies and seek their guidance

- ✔ With the power to reach virtually anyone comes greater responsibility to do your homework and respect your contacts' time

- ✔ The financials and metrics of contact campaigning are bizarre, but in a very positive way

✔ Clients have already experienced 100% response rates and ROI of 100,000% and more

✔ Considering the returns, contact campaigns are surprisingly affordable compared to most other forms of marketing

by Lee Lorenz © CartoonLink, Inc.

"Get me the ship-to-shore, Phillipe. It's time Bob Smith
learned about the power of a boat loan."

Chapter Ten

Cartoons in job search

You could say Lee Lorenz is part of the old guard in cartooning. He held the post of cartoon editor at *The New Yorker* from 1973 through 1998, was first published in the magazine in 1956 and continues to this day. But that would diminish Lee's importance as a cartoonist and as a catalyst for the development of cartooning as it exists today. As the cartoon editor, Lee was responsible for the discovery of many of the mainline cartoonists we know and cherish today. In fact, without Lee's guiding hand, we wouldn't know the work of many of the cartoonists featured in this book, or in any other publication.

I met Lee when I first started my marketing business and I couldn't have found a more helpful or gracious ally. I don't remember if I ever brought up the mistaken opinions of the direct marketing experts regarding the use of humor. But Lee certainly would have recognized their folly, because he was keenly aware of the importance and power of cartooning. I have described meeting many of my heros in cartooning in this book, and it was Lee who made many of the introductions. I owe a great deal of gratitude to Lee.

Lee is also one of the great cartoonists of our time. His boldly painted lines evoke an equally bold sense of drama in his cartoons. It's a style that stands out, which is what we want cartoons to do for our campaigns. In fact, the cartoon shown above was part of the campaign that generated a 56% response and the doubling of sales for our client, Sandoz Pharmaceuticals. You can find a large collection of Lee's work in the Cartoon Bank image bank, including every one of his cartoons published in *The New Yorker*. I highly recommend his work.

It's about standing out

This is not going to be a chapter based on formal campaigns or test results. With the exception of one position as a

marketing manager for a steel company in Los Angeles, right
after graduating from college, I have not been in the job market
for the ensuing thirty years. I have always been in business
for myself and the jobs I have found were assignments for my
marketing and creative agency. I haven't experienced the use
of Monster, CareerBuilder or HotJobs. I don't use a resumé to
sell my services, in fact, I don't even have a resumé.

I expect that nearly all of the readers of this book have
had more experience than I have in the realities of present-day
job searches, so you might conclude that I have no real advice
to offer. But I don't see it that way. Whether you own a business or work for someone else, we all sell our services. As a
business owner, I spread my income base across many clients.
As an employee, you have a single client for your services.
My company, cartoons and reputation are all part of my brand.
But you have a brand to sell as well -- you. When I seek new
clients, I use a portfolio of our most successful campaigns,
testimonial sheets, publicity, the CartoonLink.com website, and
now, this book to present my qualifications. All of which is
just another form of a resumé.

It's fitting that this chapter should follow the contact
campaigns chapter, because whether you're seeking a job or
new clients, we all have to reach and impress a decision maker
at some point. Cartoons won't help your resumé show up
more in database searches, because they don't have any effect
on a computer. But they will help you stand out to the people
involved in the decision to hire you. They can do that with
tremendous effect.

I don't have formal test results to quote concerning cartoons and job search, but I have seen them help clients stand out. Although my scope of involvement with job searches is quite limited, everyone I have helped has landed the job they were seeking. So far, we have a 100% success rate going. In some cases, a personalized cartoon was sent to the prospective employer to thank them for an interview. In once case, a BigBoard was sent to underline the candidate's desire to land the job. In all cases, they got the jobs and their new employers specifically cited the cartoon pieces as tipping factors. One told my client, "If you're clever enough to do this, we can't wait to see what you'll do for us."

The BigBoard use is particularly exciting to me, because as I mentioned in the last chapter, contact campaigning is my favorite form of marketing. It produces enormous results and even though the individual pieces aren't cheap, the return on investment potential is probably the biggest of any form of marketing. Spending a few hundred dollars is always worthwhile, whether the return comes in the form of a job or a contract, if it results in someone's investment of $100,000 or more in your personal services.

When that particular BigBoard was sent, it was to a prospective employer who wasn't convinced the candidate was capable of calling on C-level executives (CEOs, CFOs, COOs, CIOs, etc.) After receiving the piece, he was utterly convinced my client would be one of his top producers. When she next visited his office, she found the BigBoard placed right above her new employer's desk and that he referred to it often with colleagues. We are certain that the BigBoard played a big role in helping her get the job.

So we're really not so different after all. We all sell our services to one or more clients, in one form or another. And cartoons can play a major role in helping you stand out as the top candidate for any position.

Tips and resources

If you're going to put the magic of cartoons to work in your next job search, you're going to need easy-to-use resources and perhaps a bit of coaching. As you know from earlier chapters, we steer our campaigns based on the underlying truth in the cartoons we choose. For a job search, I would use a cartoon that focuses on the success of my prospective employer. I have one cartoon in the CartoonLink image bank that shows two executives seated across from one another in an office. On the wall is a sales chart with the trend line indicating a big growth in sales. The executive seated beneath the chart is looking up at it, saying to the other exec, *"You like it? I borrowed it from <Firstname> <Lastname>'s office."* That cartoon is an excellent way to pique the ego of the employer, but also an excellent opening for you to tell him or her how you're going to help further their success. I guarantee your piece will find a prominent spot in their office and that it will work as your secret weapon to stand out among your competition to help you get the job.

Some people have no sense of phone manners. I've had clients take up to six months to return phone calls, even while we have active campaigns running together. It's safe to assume there are a lot of important calls left unanswered in the realm of job searches, too. Ditto for delayed hiring decisions, all of which can be disastrous for the job seeker. Incessant calling and dozens of voicemail messages can be equally disastrous to the outcome of a prospective hiring.

But cartoons seem to be able to deliver difficult messages with impunity. When I encounter a stalled contact, I often use another of my cartoons, showing a businessman stopped at a broken-down gas station in the desert, talking on a pay phone, saying *"Hi <Firstname>, it's me again. Listen, I don't know if you've been checking your voice mail all last week, but I'm still here at the same number, waiting for your call."* What a terrific way of expressing to someone how badly their lack of phone manners has left you hanging. It almost always prompts a return call and would be perfect on a BigBoard sent to shake loose that important position you've been pursuing, but haven't been able to close.

A third use of a cartoon could focus on what would happen to the prospect's business if you're not hired. In this case, I would suggest using a non-personalized cartoon, so that you don't depict your prospective employer as a loser. In non-personalized form, a cartoon can show a situation the employer would want to avoid, without identifying him or her as the failing party. Your accompanying message could then focus on what you see as your role in helping them avoid that failure.

In Chapter 16, I list several resources you can use to spring cartoons on unsuspecting targets. You can use that section of the book as a reference, but here a few suggestions for putting cartoons to use in your job search missions.

AmazingMail/PremiumPostcard If you just want to send a quick postcard or folded greeting card with a personalized cartoon, use AmazingMail or PremiumPostcard on the web. They have a simple-to-use interface that allows you to build a card with one of our personalized cartoons. You can order one or thousands at a time and they all go in the mail the following business day. This is perfect for thanking someone for an interview or prompting them to make a decision.

CartoonLink BigBoards If you want to make a huge impression on a very important prospective employer, you can order BigBoards directly from our CartoonLink.com site. We already have formats set up with the cartoons I mentioned above, or you can have us develop a custom piece for a very special occasion. These pieces allow you to reach virtually any level in the organization, from the president or CEO on down, and certainly any key decision-makers currently deciding your fate with your target employer.

CartoonLink Members If you prefer to do your follow-up via e-mail, you can join our CartoonLink Members program, which includes a monthly newsletter, webinars and unlimited personalized cartoon e-mails (addressed and sent one at a time).

CartoonBank The CartoonBank is the place to find non-personalized cartoons, more than 150,000 of them, including seventy thousand or so that have actually appeared in *The New Yorker*.

Successories We are in the process of setting up a program with Successories that will allow you to order framed prints of a selection of non-personalized cartoons. The framed pieces can be shipped anywhere, so these will be excellent devices for thanking or making contact with a VIP employer. If the program is not yet set up, check back often. It will be worth your effort.

Advantages and disadvantages

Whether you're a business owner or an employee, we all sell our services and we all have a brand to sell. Business owners sell their services to many clients simultaneously, employees sell theirs to one client at a time. Either way, we all have to stand out to our prospective clients if we want the job. And cartoons can help us do that in a big way.

The advantage of using a cartoon in the job search mission is that it causes us to stand out among the competition, to be dominantly memorable to a prospective employer. In the end, that is what causes one person to be chosen for a position over someone else.

As with all uses of cartoons, the cartoon you use in a job search must be carefully chosen based on the truth it reveals. The safest bet is to use a personalized cartoon that casts the prospective employer as successful, while your accompanying message casts you as a necessary ingredient in their continued success.

Use the others mentioned above with some caution, because the biggest potential disadvantage of using cartoons in your job search lies in choosing the wrong message. Ask yourself, "If I was considering hiring me, what would I think of this cartoon? Would it thrill and impress me or would it turn me off?" Obviously, you want to create the strongest positive impression possible.

Key points to remember

✓ Seeking a job is no different from any other sales situation in that we always have to stand out to the person ultimately responsible for making the buying/hiring decision

✓ Cartoons can help us stand out in a big way and convince prospective employers that we're worth their investment

✓ Use cartoons to thank an employer for an interview or to initiate first contact

✓ It's easy to send one card or e-mail at a time through resources identified in this book

✓ If you want to make the biggest possible impression on a prospective employer, use one of our BigBoards to really stand out in a big way

© Edward Koren

"Well there's your problem."

Chapter Eleven

Cartoons in presentations and speeches

I met Edward Koren long ago, in a place that should be familiar to you by now in this book, the old home of *The New Yorker* on 45th Street in mid-town Manhattan. It was an exciting day, because I was there to meet Lee Lorenz, the cartoon editor of the magazine, for the first time. I quickly found Lee to be an ally in the building of my business, in that he was very generous with introductions to the other cartoonists. And that day was a bonanza.

Back in the far recesses of the fourteenth floor were individual offices cartoonists could use as their remote studios. As far as I can tell, this practice was not carried over to the present offices in the Condé Nast Building in Times Square, as everyone works from their own studios. It seemed like at any time, you might find some of the world's finest cartoonists hard at work in those musty back offices back then, which is exactly what was happening that day.

Luckily for me, one of those cartoonists working in the back rooms was Edward Koren. I'd admired his work for a long time, as he had been published in the magazine since 1962. His drawings are immediately identifiable by the wooly, broken lines that form the characters, almost as though you're looking at an impressionist painting. You don't have to squint to see the genius in his work, though. You just can't help but fall in love with those scratchy, off-kilter characters he casts in his cartoons. So it was a great thrill for me to meet the man behind the exquisite drawings I'd been seeing for so long.

Even if you aren't a regular reader of *The New Yorker*, it's very likely his work is familiar, having appeared in *Newsweek*, *Time*, *New York Times*, *GQ*, *Esquire*, *Sports Illustrated*, *Vogue*, *Vanity Fair*, *The Nation* and the *Boston Globe*. He has also published several children's books and occasionally makes appearances at art shows and retrospectives in his honor.

Mr. Koren's work is also found in abundance in the Cartoon Bank, awaiting your use. I guarantee it will add a lot of visual interest to your presentations, projects and campaigns, and worth your investment.

Get ready to shine

Great presentations can move mountains. They can change the fortunes of your company, open new doors, or generate new sales. Presentations that connect with the audience can create support for an idea or simply entertain, whether it is an audience of one or thousands, in person or via the Internet. If you have the ability to give a great presentation at a moment's notice, it can change your life.

Most people seem to find the idea of speaking to a large audience terrifying. Trainers tell us stage fright is a natural, yet irrational fear of being judged, and they have taught many of us to ignore it and go on with the show. But what about the fear of boring our audience? I think that is one fear we ought to heed.

Because as a reader of this book, you already know how to make your presentations stand out and convey your message powerfully. With cartoons, of course. As in many other missions described in this book, assuming you've done a good job choosing cartoons that convey the right effect, they will delight your audience and lead them wherever you want to go.

As a cartoonist, I rarely get to see the reaction my cartoons produce, which is why I enjoy presenting to large groups. There is nothing more satisfying than to put a few cartoons up on the screen and have your audience laughing along with you. And as a reader of this book, you know that their laughter signifies their agreement with your points. It all combines to create a very persuasive and entertaining effect.

When planning your presentation, I recommend using a mix of personalized and non-personalized cartoons. Your choice of cartoons needs to support your points and draw attention to the dramatic transitions in your speech, and you can spin interesting effects with the audience with an occasional cartoon personalized with the name of someone present and known to the entire group. The balance between personalized versus non-personalized cartoons depends mostly on the size of the group. The larger the group, the fewer personalized cartoons I would suggest using. I think there is a risk that some audience members in larger groups won't know the person mentioned in the caption. In a small group sitting around a meeting table, I suggest shifting the mixture to mostly personalized cartoons.

The benefit a non-personalized cartoon brings to a presentation is that it conveys a point of agreement fairly universally. Personalized cartoons do that as well, but their impact is focused on a single person. In smaller groups, I have seen fellow attendees laugh simply because the person in the caption is right there to share the gag. That effect tends to dilute as the audience gets bigger.

A speaker's advice

Jay Marks is an organizational consultant who really gets it about cartoons. He has been licensing cartoons from the Cartoon Bank for the past twenty five years, injecting them into every corner of his presentations. In fact, he goes way beyond what I usually do.

I was introduced to Jay recently and as we were talking, it occurred to me that he is the prototype of what I hope all readers of this book will become. He understands how cartoons evoke truth and he uses those points of agreement constantly in his sales and training presentations. His presentations don't remain static, because his points change as his business progresses and as he addresses new audiences. So his collection of licensed images constantly shifts as well, based on the message he is conveying at the time.

Not all presentations are made on a screen, and I particularly admire how Jay uses cartoons in his printed handouts. Some of his printed presentations are nothing more than a series of cartoons, one to a page, each directed at making a certain point along the way. He emerges from these with a full understanding of his points and full agreement from his audience. I can't wait to try that myself.

Knowing what you now know about how cartoons work and how to use them in your projects, imagine what you can accomplish with a renewed commitment to producing entertaining presentations that educate, promote and sell.

Advantages and disadvantages

Presentations that are entertaining and persuasive are literally just a few clicks away, with an inexhaustible supply of personalized cartoons from CartoonLink and non-personalized cartoons, many of which were published in *The New Yorker,* from the Cartoon Bank.

The ability to put on a compelling presentation has always been valuable, but it's even more so now, because there are so many more speaking opportunities. Speakers used to have to travel many weeks out of the year to pack in enough seminar and trade show dates. These were tough spots to get, expensive to support, and the events required attendees to spend just as much to get there, before they ever bought a thing. Webinars have changed that dynamic tremendously, opening many more opportunities to give presentations that help you and your company. Events no longer require anyone to invest time and expense in travel, and most are free to attend.

Whatever form your presentation takes, you now know how to integrate cartoons into your speeches to lend them a lot more impact. You can even make your entire printed presentation just a series of cartoons if you want.

As with all other missions discussed in this book, you'll need to choose your cartoons carefully, focusing on aligning the underlying truth of the humor with each point of your message. There are a lot of advantages to being able to make effective, entertaining presentations whenever the opportunity arises and cartoons give you that ability with ease.

Disadvantages? Sure, and they're all tied to how carefully you choose your cartoons and if you mess with the captions. It's advice I have explained in the early chapters and included throughout the book. Choose cartoons that illustrate your points based on their underlying truths. And never change the caption to inject your brand, offer or identity.

Key points to remember

- ✔ Great presentations can change the fortunes of companies and those who give them

- ✔ Everyone feels stage fright, so don't let yours keep you from making presentations

- ✔ The biggest mistake you could make is to bore your audience

- ✔ Anyone can give an entertaining and persuasive presentation, just by including the right cartoons

- ✔ As with other missions in this book, be sure to choose your cartoons carefully

- ✔ Don't mess with the captions and never make alterations to inject your brand, product, service, offer or identity

- ✔ Webinars have changed the speaking landscape, offering you and potential audiences far more opportunities to connect through your presentations

© Roz Chast

Chapter Twelve

Cartoons in publicity and social media

I don't know Roz Chast, but I admire her work tremendously, which makes me one of the millions who have enjoyed her more than 800 cartoons published in *The New Yorker*, plus many more seen in *Harvard Business Review*, *Scientific American* and the *Village Voice*.

As with many of the cartoonists whose work is found in *The New Yorker*, Roz's drawings stand out as unique among many of the world's great magazine gag cartoonists, but that is nearly an understatement in her case. Her whimsical style incorporates somewhat hidden gag elements throughout; in Roz's drawings, such normally inconsequential things as intricate wallpaper or tiny tchotchkes found on side tables, even the furniture become part of the cast of characters.

The writing of her gags is also quite different from what the rest of us do in our cartoons. When I create a cartoon, for instance, I'm building toward a sudden reveal, something that makes you laugh because it is entirely unexpected. Roz's gags are a more subtle form that combines a narrative layer over the comments of characters caught in everyday, yet absurd circumstances. It's difficult to explain, but joyfully experienced when viewed.

Roz's work can be licensed for a number of uses from the CartoonBank, which is very good. Just seeing her work will draw attention and lend credibility to your projects and campaigns.

Publicity uses

Are you ready to become famous? Or just to draw a bit of attention to your company, product or service? The right publicity in the right amount can change your fortunes overnight. If you're known to and admired by a large segment of the population, that's worth a lot in terms of making your career or company move into high gear.

Have you ever watched the people standing outside the broadcast studio for those network morning shows? I think they look silly. They're standing there, waving to the camera, holding their signs that broadcast some aspect of their lives no one could possibly care about -- *It's our 23rd anniversary! Hi mom!* -- and they're thrilled to be spilling their personal details on national TV. There is a rather large segment of the population for whom fame is the ultimate goal, but sadly, they have nothing to offer an audience and they have no idea they're required to do so. They see the "trappings" of fame, the constant recognition and attention lavished by strangers and it triggers a deep-seated need to be accepted, noticed and loved. These are the worst possible candidates for publicity, because there is no substance behind their desire for notoriety. They fail to recognize the real trapping of fame which is that you're stuck inside a bubble where no one respects your privacy, where you can never go out and do anything anonymously.

These are not the people I have in mind when writing this section. If you are ready to become famous because your talent or business requires it, then I have an interesting solution for you. You know what it is -- using a cartoon to help you accomplish your mission.

Cartoons draw attention from all sorts of people. Cartoons convey a point more effectively than just about anything you could put on a printed surface. In personalized form, cartoons draw recipients in and generate instant goodwill. Good. You'll need all of that when trying to get publicity, because it isn't easy. Reporters, editors and producers are a tough crowd. They're cynical and very hard to impress. But they're still people and most people enjoy a good cartoon.

So I can see several uses for cartoons in a publicity campaign. First, just as a way to draw the attention of an editor or producer, sending a well-targeted cartoon is an excellent device for reaching past their reservations toward strangers. As I seek publicity for this book, you can count on my use of our BigBoards to pull me through. I'm sure the contact boards will help me reach people that would otherwise be beyond my grasp, as usual.

Still, while editors may be swayed by a surprising piece showing up at their offices, they're too cynical to let it pass without putting it to the "is this just a gimmick?" test. That's where your training in this book makes a critical difference, because you know you've got to choose a cartoon carefully, based on its underlying truth and how it supports your central point.

So assuming the cartoon used in your publicity campaign is well targeted, the next step is to offer its use as part of the story. Now that is something an editor might find interesting, because it just made their job easier. You've just supplied an important piece of the content they'll need to tell your story. Again, you can count on seeing that form of use in my own publicity efforts. So if you see some of my cartoons showing up in a story about this book or about CartoonLink, you'll know it's working.

If your planned use of the cartoon includes editorial publication, you'll need to set up a special license to include that usage. In that case, see if you can negotiate a per-publication usage, so you only pay if an editor wants it, and only if they take your story. I think it creates an effective incentive to get an editor to look favorably on your pitch.

Social Media uses

I have to admit, I just didn't catch on to the marketing potential of social media until just recently. I understand that Facebook, Twitter and the other networks have a lot of traffic in aggregate, but seeing Joe's Pizzeria on the corner setting up Twitter and Facebook pages seemed about as useful as Pizza Joe posting his flyers in his own bathroom at home. No one other than Joe sees it and no one cares. Yet most of the major corporations are throwing money at social media.

But then I started listening to Doug Schust, a wizard at social media marketing, and I started to see what the attraction is. And then I met Andrew Fowler and the flood gates started to budge. Doug showed me how gaining buzz in social media networks can greatly affect your site's search rankings, which does translate into value and one hopes, new business. Then Andrew explained how he has been using cartoons to create a large volume of buzz using cartoons.

Andrew's story is an interesting one. He doesn't actually draw, but he thoroughly understands how cartoons work and how to write an effective gag. His art is an assemblage of clip art downloaded from free sources on the Web, so he doesn't need to draw. In fact, the clip art look has become his style of "drawing" and it works.

Mashable just named Andrew the fourth most circulated cartoonist in social media. The way he got there is amazing, but what he discovered he could do with it is certainly an inspiration to me. And it's a trick we can all use, now that you understand how to choose and target cartoons. Andrew reasoned that most nodes in the social mediasphere were getting very little traffic (like Pizza Joe's Twitter and Facebook pages), but there were a few giants as well. So he started sending targeted cartoons to bloggers with large followings, including one of the founders of Twitter. They responded in kind, by including the cartoon in their posts, creating a link back to Andrew's site. Okay, if a cartoon will cause someone with a large audience to place a link back to your site, that is a big deal and possibly worth a lot in terms of new business.

Andrew suggests setting up the linked cartoon on a landing page that includes an offer, or perhaps a link to take visitors to your Web site. I think this has to be done carefully, so that it does not come across as misleading, because it will turn off the referring party and turn the audience against you. But there definitely is intriguing value here.

Doug Schust is CEO of M3 SocialMindz, an international social marketing media agency based in Toronto, and the veteran of many social media campaigns for some of the world's biggest marketers, including Sony, Trader Vic's, Mitsubishi and more. He likes Andrew's cartoon link idea, but cautions that you shouldn't over commercialize the effort. If you're going to lead visitors to a landing page, for instance, make sure there is plenty of value that is not tied to the sponsor. Setting up the page so that users can forward the same cartoon personalized to friends is a viable way to create favor, traffic and a viral spread of your campaign. At the same time, there's nothing wrong with having a set of links to coupons or some other offer form, which provides value to the sponsor.

Advantages and disadvantages

Cartoons get attention from everyone, and that includes editors, producers, reporters and social media mavens. But these are a special class of people; they have enormous audiences and have the power to either make you look good or foolish. They will do that based on the feeling they get about you. If you come across as genuine and fascinating, they want to be among the first to report your story. If they think anything is slightly off -- whether it actually is or is not -- they can conjure some pretty negative stuff to say about you, and if that will boost ratings or sell more issues, they will take you down.

So you must be 100% honest, first with yourself about your motivations for seeking this sort of mass attention, next on whether your story is interesting enough to excite them to action. In providing details of your story, you must also be entirely honest, because they will find out if you're not. Lawyers may start with the presumption of innocence, but journalists assume you're lying and uninteresting until you convince them otherwise.

Assuming you're still interested, there is a whole world out there waiting for interesting new faces and stories. Every media outlet relies on experts to fill out a story, like the experts you've seen countless times on television and in print. You could be one of them. The media is always looking for the next new trend and you could either be part of that -- or starting your own. In that case, they'll be all over your story.

Cartoons certainly are a device to get that kind of attention from the media, but you have to choose them carefully and set up a license that allows for specific publication rights. If you think about it, there really isn't much difference between mainstream media and social media. Both can give you tremendous visibility which can translate into higher search rankings, more business and ultimately, more money in your pocket.

The apparent disadvantages in the use of cartoons for this set of missions stem from choosing a cartoon that does not reflect the actual truth about you, your talent, product or company. A poorly-targeted cartoon may leave this audience in particular, unhappy with you, and they have the platform to convey their displeasure to a large audience. So don't disappoint or anger them.

If I have painted a bleak or scary picture, consider this: I will be out there using my tools (cartoons) to get my name out there, generate traffic to the CartoonLink web site and, of course, to talk about this book. I believe in the power of publicity and am coming around quickly regarding social media. It's high on my agenda for the foreseeable future and if you have a compelling story to tell, or special expertise that can enrich people's lives, you should be pursuing publicity and social media buzz, too.

Key points to remember

- ✓ Publicity is about people with compelling stories to tell, but fame in itself is not a real goal

- ✓ Editors, producers and reporters are tough-minded and difficult to reach, which is the perfect mission for using cartoons

- ✓ Cartoons can be used as attention devices and as part of the content for your story

- ✓ When using cartoons for publicity or social media, be sure to arrange re-publication usage in your license

- ✓ Cartoons can also be used to bring enormous visibility and traffic through social media

Please don't forget to claim your free "Stu Heinecke Dingbats" font at http://www.CartoonLink.com/claim_font

by Anne Gibbons © CartoonLink, Inc.

"Let's see if Sarah wants to join us for some serious whining and dining!"

Chapter Thirteen

Cartoons and nonprofits

While she is not part of *The New Yorker* family, Anne Gibbons is an accomplished cartoonist, and one of six women cartoonists who create the "SixChix" cartoon strip syndicated by King Features to more than 120 newspapers. She has also been a part of the CartoonLink family since 2000, when Arnie Levin introduced us.

Back then, we were experimenting with publishing a weekly set of cartoon features, using our personalization techniques, and we'd gotten up to about 50,000 subscribers before ending the run. The experiment was a terrific success, thanks in part to Anne's regular weekly cartoons on women's issues.

We learned a number of lessons and clearly saw the potential for editorial use of personalized cartoons, but there were some mishaps. Many of those were tied to Anne's cartoons, though they were never her fault. Although we warned readers her cartoons were strictly for women, there were always males in the audience who would complain that they'd been improperly pegged as female in the captions. It reminds me of the original Web site for L'Eggs, which held your browser captive until you submitted your height and weight and it told you what size pantyhose to wear. If you were in the wrong place, well, you should have known going in.

When it concluded, the CartoonLink weekly e-mail was tremendously popular and helped us see how personalized cartoons could sustain monstrous open rates, even with weekly frequency of publication. These will surely show up in some of the tablet magazines planned for launch from our incubator venture.

In the meantime, it gave us a terrific opportunity to get to know and appreciate Anne's sensibilities as a cartoonist. I'm glad to say we have quite a few personalized cartoons by Anne in our own CartoonLink image bank, ready for use in your campaigns.

Are cartoons appropriate for nonprofits?

This will be counter-intuitive for many readers, but I have found cartoons to be entirely appropriate for use in non-profit campaigns. Since most of these organizations deal with deadly serious diseases or tragic circumstances somewhere in the world, how could humor possibly be useful, tasteful or appropriate? Wouldn't the use of humor kill a donor acquisition campaign and create ruinous publicity for the charitable organization?

The answer to these questions certainly surprised me, until I took a fresh look after several conversations with my old friend, Linus Shackelford. Linus had approached me several times over the years, asking about having a campaign created for his funeral business. When I'd been asked during speeches if I thought cartoons were ever inappropriate, my response had always been, "There are always human experiences tied to every product or service, so I can't see there ever being a time when cartoons wouldn't be a powerful tool to influence an audience," I would say, "with the exception of something like funeral homes or something dealing with a deadly disease, like cancer."

But Linus pressed on, explaining that often, his patrons wanted to focus on the positive rather than the negative in their ceremonies. The survivors would almost always tell him, "We want this to be a celebration of our loved one's life, not their death." He showed me that even a highly negative situation has a positive side.

He challenged my thinking, and eventually, I got it. People donate to the American Cancer Society because they want to have a hand in curing the disease. Suddenly, everywhere I looked, that same solution presented itself. People want to make a difference. It is a universal human experience that can certainly breed humor and agreement that the disease must be stamped out or the people in the tragic circumstance must be helped. If people are given the opportunity, most want to be part of the solution, and that is exactly what nonprofit campaigns are about. They provide an easy way for people to help others and do good in the world.

Linus and I never did do that campaign together, but his prods helped me sort this out. Even when humor seems to be utterly ruled out, there always seems to be a way to make it work quite powerfully.

The breakthrough campaigns

Fortunately, this discussion developed well beyond my enlightening conversations with Linus, with several breakthrough campaigns to show for it. Each one is fascinating to me, because I still look at them and think, "humor just shouldn't fit here, but it's actually working quite well."

If you check Chapter 5, you'll find a few of those campaigns described. One was an on-sert applied to the final issue of *Arthritis Today*, the membership magazine of the Arthritis Foundation, making one last attempt to get lapsing members to renew their annual donation. There is nothing funny about arthritis, but there was plenty of room for humor in their appeal for renewed donations, and as a result, my cartoon piece became their new control and remained in that spot for fifteen years. That's an extraordinary result; in direct marketing, it's like winning the Superbowl fifteen years in a row.

On that same page in Chapter 5, I also described a campaign we did for the American Diabetes Association, which did not beat their control, but remains an excellent example of an effective use of humor in a serious, nonprofit solicitation. I created a multi-panel cartoon that used a font of my chicken-scratch handwriting to fill in recipients' names within the quote bubbles in the artwork. And the gag was about wanting to make a difference, but never having received the right thing in the mail to make that happen. The copy inside told the reader, "you just received the right thing in the mail to make your difference." This test probably suffered from using a more expensive format, and I would be curious to see what it would do in a more comparable package to their control. Or perhaps turn it into an e-mail campaign. I'm sure it still has plenty of potential to become their winning package.

I have also produced strong results when the humor is aimed at membership in nonprofits. Although I am not allowed to mention them by name, I can report that one of our tests beat a member-acquisition control for a nonprofit that is one of the top five biggest mailers in the U.S. Although I have worked with many very sophisticated marketers, this client is the most advanced user of statistics and testing I have ever encountered. Beating one of their controls is an enormous confirmation that humor does indeed belong in the nonprofit marketer's toolbox.

Advantages and disadvantages

Although I've been convinced that cartoons can play a big part in nonprofit marketing missions, this is one instance where I would advise extreme caution. There are usually very serious issues tied to nonprofit organizations, and the big danger is that the humor can miss the target pretty easily. You obviously don't want to be mailing something that makes fun of cancer patients or light of the disease.

More than any other topic covered in this book, there is more risk involved with nonprofit campaigns than any other type for something to go very wrong with the use of humor. On the other hand, we have already shown that humor does work extremely well in these missions, when created with a delicate sense of portraying the recipient as someone who can make a difference if given the chance. I've done it several times and it works.

Major donors also deserve attention for their generous help. A BigBoard with any of the cartoons mentioned in this section would be a terrific way to thank your top donors, while standing out all year long in their offices or dens at home.

As with all other uses of cartoons, you will need to focus on the underlying truth of the cartoon, rather than injecting your brand, as a way to steer the humor properly. In nonprofit campaigns, just as in commercial campaigns, focusing the cartoon on your brand is likely to kill the effect and produce disappointing results.

Key points to remember

✔ It would seem cartoons are not appropriate for nonprofit mailings, but experience has already proven this to be false

✔ For nonprofit campaigns dealing with serious diseases or tragic events, humor must focus on giving the recipient a chance to make a difference

✔ We have already created personalized cartoon campaigns that have surpassed tough controls, including one that served as control for fifteen years

✔ Using humor in nonprofit campaigns requires an extra measure of caution to ensure it is carefully directed

✔ As with all other uses of cartoons, focus on the underlying truth of the cartoon, rather than injecting your brand, to properly target the humor

✔ BigBoards could be an excellent way to thank major donors while standing out all year long in their offices or dens

by Stu Heinecke © CartoonLink, Inc.

"*Sorry, Bob. The music stopped, you didn't find a chair, you're fired.*"

Chapter Fourteen

Cartoons in social situations

I've been introducing all of my heros of cartooning in previous chapters, but I haven't told you anything about myself as a cartoonist. A lot of people ask how someone gets started in cartooning. For me, it started with a lot of doodling on desks in school, coupled with my aforementioned misadventures reading *Playboy* and other magazines as a kid. I had always marveled at the way these simple drawings told so much, how they conveyed an entire story instantly. I think everyone starts at that point, whether they're destined to be a cartoonist or not.

All of my heros of cartooning have had their own heros from the generation before. You've already met mine in this book, and I hope I am helping to inspire the next generation of cartoonists to come. If I am, there will be a lot more mixing of business and mischief with cartooning.

I didn't get serious about cartooning until after my final year in college. A good friend at the time had been telling me about a cartooning class he was taking from Eric Teitelbaum, also an occasional contributor to *The New Yorker*. My friend -- we'll call him Dick -- would tell me about guest speakers, including Lee Lorenz at one point, the then cartoon editor for *The New Yorker* and one of the cartoonists featured in this book. After one particular class, Dick told me about a guest lecture by the art director for a locally-produced magazine, who made it seem a pretty simple task to sell cartoons at eighty dollars apiece. He referred to the art director as "Chada," and I had been so fired up by Dick's account of the class, that I decided to call him myself. I figured it would be easy money, like writing myself $80 checks at will. Man, was I way off.

The next day, I called the magazine and asked for "Chada," which caused the switchboard operator some distress, but she finally put me through. "Is this Chada?" I asked. A rather irritated voice on the other end responded, "This is <u>Jim</u> Chada, who are you?"

That was the end of writing checks to myself and the start of some serious work to bring my cartooning up to par. Cartooning is an endeavor that includes a lot of rejection. It's a gauntlet very few aspiring cartoonists run and survive, and those who do become immune to its effect. It often becomes fodder for our humor, at least among ourselves. So I survived that challenge, at first selling cartoons for five dollars apiece to a local advertiser. The tiny amount didn't bother me, all that mattered was that I was being paid to cartoon. From there, I moved up to cartooning and illustrating for the *Los Angeles Herald Examiner* and the in-flight magazine for one of the airlines. I was on my way.

You'll recall that I have always had a dual career in cartooning and marketing, and at this point, I held the title of marketing manager for a steel distributor in Los Angeles. It was a natural progression to start experimenting with cartoons in the weekly mail campaign I managed for my employer. The more information I read about cartooning, particularly their performance in editorial readership surveys, the more encouraged I became to develop the story you already know from this book.

One of the things that has always amazed me, as I have built the CartoonLink business, is how well my cartoons have blended with the other styles offered through our service. The other cartoonists featured in the CartoonLink service are my heros, some of the best in the world at what they do. I have always left it up to my clients as to whose work they wanted to use in their campaigns, and was surprised to see mine chosen so often. I suspect that has to do with my background, having created so many winning campaigns, including having drawn many of the featured cartoons myself. I'm quite proud of my work as a cartoonist and always happy to get involved in helping a client solve a marketing challenge.

Cartooning in public places

I've taken you through some pretty serious missions in this book, from using cartoons in marketing, advertising and sales promotion to more personal uses to help you secure a new job, make better presentations and gain notoriety through publicity and social media. Now it's time to have some fun with cartooning, if you're up to the task.

There was a time in my life when I found myself suddenly single again. Although I enjoy being married, this was a fascinating time of discovery, misadventure and just plain fun, and it all stemmed from using cartoons in a most unusual way. I can't even remember how it started, but I quickly discovered that if I drew a cartoon on a bar napkin and sent it to a particularly interesting woman in a restaurant or at a bar, I always seemed to get a great reaction and it opened the door for a friendly conversation. I was seeing the effect of cartoons firsthand, which was a lot of fun for me, because cartoonists hardly ever get to see audiences react to their work.

Every single guy needs a good wingman and I found the best. A mutual friend introduced me to Jay Silverman, a crazy photographer and commercial director based in Hollywood. Sandra thought we would get along well, and we did. Jay suggested we get together for dinner at a restaurant in Venice Beach to talk shop, since we both had rapidly-rising advertising businesses. At one point during dinner, I said, "Jay, watch this," and I drew a quick cartoon on a napkin and had it delivered via waiter to three women sitting at the bar.

The cartoon was rather obnoxious, but I already knew that it would be well-received -- or so I thought. Meanwhile, Jay was thoroughly embarrassed. "Stu, don't do it, don't send that!" he said, but I assured him it would yield surprising results. But the more we sat there, the more it seemed these women had ignored us. So I told Jay I'd be right back, that I wanted to retrieve the cartoon so I could send it to someone else who would appreciate it. Now Jay was wondering what kind of lunatic our friend Sandra had introduced him to. "Stu, leave it alone," he pleaded, but I went anyway. When I got there, I asked if they still had the cartoon because they had obviously ignored it and now I wanted it back.

But they hadn't ignored it all. In fact, they were busy drawing up a reply, which would be finished and delivered momentarily. When I got back to the table and explained the situation to Jay, he was hooked. From then on, Jay and I would get together and cartoon in restaurants. He was a madman with a terrific -- and perfectly undeveloped -- style of cartooning.

For some reason, many of his characters sported a big, toothy sneer with a smoldering match clenched between their teeth, as though they'd lit a cigarette and smoked the wrong thing. We became instantly popular in any restaurant we visited, but always wanted to preserve the element of surprise in our escapades, so we hated having people come up to us, asking for a cartoon portrait of themselves. In those situations, I would explain that it would be okay produce the drawing, but I wanted my protégé to do it, because he was still learning. Jay would then go to work drawing these people with that same giant sneer and smoldering match in their teeth. We always seemed to send them away a bit bewildered by the new souvenir they had just acquired.

Although we hit a lot of restaurants, we settled in on a favorite, a place called Rebecca's in Venice Beach, just a few blocks away from Jay's house on the canals. Rebecca's was the scene of many great times using cartoons on napkins as our form of entertainment. By then, our mode of operation became streamlined; pick out someone in the restaurant, draw a quick cartoon and have the waiter deliver it. It had become such a production line, that at one point, one of our guests couldn't help laughing at what was happening. A cartoon would go out, the woman would come over, and we were already sending one out to someone else. Meanwhile, they would stand there, wondering what just happened.

Rebecca's was also the setting for two very interesting events in our social cartooning careers. By sending the cartoons around the restaurant, Jay and I usually would meet everybody there. One evening, as we were drawing away, we noticed everyone in the restaurant was suddenly sending cartoons to each other -- it had caught on throughout the dining room and bar. It was fascinating to sit back and watch it all happen.

At one point, *Playboy* heard about our adventures and asked if they could have one of their writers tag along on one of our cartooning sessions at Rebecca's. What an evening that was. As we sat in our booth explaining how bar napkin cartooning works, the reporter would direct us to send cartoons to various people in the place. His first target was three women having dinner together. "Those are Venice women over there, they have a wall fourteen feet tall around them, you'll never get through." We did and they ended up joining us at the table. Then he pointed out a couple on a date and said, "Send one to her," thinking the guy would come over and give us a punch. But we knew better, because we'd already seen how much couples enjoy the attention. "Okay," he said, exasperatedly, "send one to those two women and let's see what happens." They rushed over to the table, "Oh it's you guys again! We have the last cartoon you sent framed at our house!"

I never saw the story he wrote, but he muttered something about Jay and me being the ultimate pick-up artists. But that wasn't at all what we were up to. Social cartooning became simply a great form of entertainment for us and for our "victims." We tried sending cartoons to women first, then to couples on dates and finally, to large groups, which seemed to be the most entertaining from our perspective. They would

invite us to their parties, buy us drinks and food and just involve us in their fun.

There were also times when we would try this as a
technique for business lunches, to take clients out cartooning.
That turned out to be a difficult proposition, because it requires
concentration and means that you spend a lot of your time
ignoring one another. I did this once with a client from *The
Atlantic Magazine* in a little restaurant in Manhattan, thinking
that if she saw the reactions I could generate there, she would
gladly buy in on a new campaign for the magazine. So I sent a
cartoon to a couple of women across the room from us. One of
them came over and asked if she knew me. "No, I don't think
we do," I responded. "Oh, okay. We thought you might have
been someone we rejected for a book deal." It turned out these
were the two people responsible for publishing B. Kliban's
best-selling trilogy of cartoon books, *Cat, Never Eat Anything
Bigger Than Your Head* and *Whack Your Porcupine*. You just
never know who you'll meet in restaurants, and amazing opportunities abound in these places to make terrific connections.

So, now it's your turn.

If you're going to try this, remember that it's going to
start out being rather scary, but stick with it. Don't do it on
your own, find a great friend like I did in Jay, because you'll
need the support at first, and you'll need someone to laugh with
later as you see the hilarity kick in. Don't draw on the restaurant's fine linen napkins or table cloths (this happened one
night when while entertaining one of the top officials from the

U.S. Postal Service and things really got out of hand). Always use the double-fold, standard bar napkin for your cartoons, and always have the waiter deliver them to their target. And remember to have fun. If someone ignores your cartoon, ask for it back, because they're being rude and don't deserve to be included in the entertainment.

The social cartoonist's tools

If you're going to give the bar napkin routine a try, you'll need a few tools to get started. Let's assume the restaurant or bar already has the right kind of napkins. If not, complain and find another place. Next, you'll need a good set of pens. My favorites are the standard rolling-writer kinds of gel pens, black ink only. Next, you'll need a few variations of gray markers to shade the drawings, making them more readable and somewhat more polished. You'll find these at any artist supply store, or try DickBlick.com. While you're at it, see if you can find a handy case to keep your tools organized and in one easy-to-find place.

You have a choice to caption your drawings using comic book-style bubbles or with text centered across the bottom of the napkin. I suggest using the balloons, because they're easier to plan and can show the characters either talking or thinking something to themselves. Captions should be kept as short as possible so you can fit some art into the cartoon. Start out by writing what you want in the balloons, then fill in the drawing around the captions. The scenes and characters should always be of the people you're targeting and of that moment. That is what will make the cartoons so endearing to the recipients, because it is a drawing of them, right then and there.

A few gags to start you off

So, what sort of gags should you use? Well, keep in mind this is flirtation, so be bold and somewhat obnoxious, but oddly, you don't have to be too worried about being witty. The psychology of these cartoons is different from the ones you'll use in all of the other missions described in this book. In campaigns, the cartoon can never picture the recipient because it's impossible; in social cartooning, you should always picture the recipient in the drawing. And because they are the star of the cartoon, they're already won over. Add a bit of spicy mischief and you have the makings of a very successful bar napkin cartoon.

I once overheard someone use as a pick-up line at a bar, *"I'd like to express my interest in you."* I thought it was hilarious and it certainly could be construed to have a double and very sexual meaning. It forms the basis for a very obnoxious cartoon on a napkin. In my use, I showed a guy making a gesture to illustrate his intentions as he delivered the line to the woman at the bar, and it always seemed to be well-received. That taught me that people will give you get a lot of leeway in the level of obnoxiousness allowed in gags.

I would often show two women sitting together having their meal, with one exuberantly proclaiming, *"Oh Fiona -- may I call you Fiona? --"* and then finish it with something I've noticed about the other woman, like, *"I love your new coat!"* or *"your new haircut is the best!"* Sometimes I'd finish the caption with something completely from left field, like *"I'm so sorry your rat died."* Another favorite showed a fisherman holding a big fish in his arms, standing over their table saying, *"Hi ladies, caught this just for you."* The trick was to have an anchovy handy from my meal, which I draped across the fisherman, so it became his presented catch.

There are many others, but use your imagination and come up with a few of your own. Just keep it fun for you and the recipients and watch what happens as a result. You'll be amazed at what unfolds and where it leads you.

My wife is from Denmark and her father was knighted by Queen Margrethe. So it has long been my ambition to break through to her and take the royals out cartooning. Sadly, my father-in-law is no longer with us and cartooning has taken on a new meaning lately in Denmark, perhaps making it too much of a security risk to hit a few bars together. But you never know. The Queen is an accomplished artist and far more accessible to her people than, say, Queen Elizabeth is to her subjects. And cartoons have lead me to some pretty surprising places already. That would be the ultimate experience of drawing cartoons on bar napkins.

Cartoons as gifts

Cartooning in restaurants requires a bit of skill and it puts you on the spot in a most delightful way, but even I recognize it's not for everyone. That's okay, because you can still use cartoons very effectively in social situations, as gifts.

I don't know why magazine gag cartooning hasn't taken off as collectible or investment art. As you know from reading this book, cartoons are supremely popular among readers, so it would make sense that these same people would covet the original works, but so far, single-panel magazine cartoons remain the runts of the art world. I find that especially odd, because of what has happened to the markets for animation cells and comic book art, which have soared in value. You'll pay several thousand dollars to buy an animation "cell" that may have been mass-produced and may not have even been part of the movie. A recent listing of an R. Crumb comic book cover illustration sold for $36,000. But you can buy the original art of cartoons that have appeared in *The New Yorker* for just over a thousand dollars.

As a wedding present, Leo Cullum gave my wife and me the original of his *"Men Working Things Out"* cartoon which appeared in the magazine, and it is something we will treasure the rest of our lives. Similarly, if you have someone very special or important that you want to surprise with a gift that will leave an impact, giving an original from *The New Yorker* or just a framed print, perhaps even of a personalized cartoon, will be a big hit, guaranteed.

Buying cartoons as gifts is easy. You can contact *The New Yorker* directly to buy originals. I have listed several galleries in Chapter 16 that specialize in gag cartoon originals as well. The Cartoon Bank sells framed prints of any cartoon in their image bank, and you can buy from a selection of customizable, framed CartoonLink prints from Successories.

Key points to remember

- ✓ Cartooning on napkins in bars and restaurants is a powerful way to meet everyone there

- ✓ Social cartoons can be far more obnoxious than you might expect and still be very successful

- ✓ Start out with a friend, for support, collaboration and to share the fun

- ✓ Be bold; this is scary at first, but fully worth the effort

- ✓ It is more important for social cartoons to be personalized and mischievous than witty

- ✓ Go forth and see what kinds of connections develop

"I used to be a turnaround specialist, now I'm a meltdown specialist."

Chapter Fifteen

Words of caution

Throughout this book, I have introduced you to some of the world's finest single-panel gag cartoonists. Admittedly, there is a bias toward mostly American cartoonists because they are the ones I know. Cartooning and humor are a truly universal language and there are surely amazing cartoonists in every developed culture, in every country in the world, so it may be a bit of a stretch to call my choices the very best, but I believe they actually are.

I did this as a form of training for you. If you're going to use cartoons in your projects and campaigns, you need to become a discerning buyer. Incorporating the works of some of the finest cartoonists in the world is easy and not too terribly expensive, and it lends respectability to your own work. It serves as a form of celebrity endorsement of you, your company or your products. Their work will make you look good.

That is in stark contrast to many of the imitator efforts I've seen so far, particularly in the direct marketing arena, where the amateurs are just as happy to use "Bob in the back room," because he draws funny pictures. As a reader of this book, you now know there is some much more to a cartoon than a funny drawing, and you've now been introduced to some of my all-time favorites. Please use that knowledge to be smart enough to rebuff any calls to substitute back-room Bob's drawings for real cartoons by real cartoonists who understand how to make a cartoon funny, poignant and relevant to your mission.

You can't navigate the streets of Detroit with a map of Chicago

When I talk about the "experts" and how they derided the use of cartoons, I always have to qualify my comments, because they were partially right. If you don't know what you're doing, it is nearly impossible to use humor well, and when humor is done poorly, it fails spectacularly. So let's give them credit. At least the "experts" recognized that they weren't qualified to make humor work. Their mistake was in thinking no one could ever be qualified to unleash the incredible power of humor in campaigns and more.

But you know differently. You have far more knowledge now on the subject than they ever did.

I once had an assignment to create a mail campaign for AT&T. The client loved our work and the thinking behind our concepts, so they directed their agency to work with us to develop a new campaign. And that agency hated us for it. I have never seen so much energy poured into discrediting a collaborator. At one point, their art buyer went behind my back to Leo Cullum, the cartoonist from our team whose work would appear in the campaign. She came back with a report to the client, saying that we were charging twenty times more than the price she had just obtained directly from Leo. Of course, Leo had no idea she was talking about the AT&T campaign -- she never even identified herself as the art buyer from the agency -- and he gave her a rate for using a cartoon in a small-circulation newsletter. It was a dirty trick.

In response, I wrote a four-page essay about the value of our involvement, based on steering the campaign according to our test experience. What I said was, the agency lacked this expertise and was blindly sabotaging the campaign. I titled the whole thing, *You Can't Navigate the Streets of Detroit with a Map of Chicago*, and it hit the mark precisely with the client. The campaign went on to become the most successful piece ever mailed for that product from AT&T.

This is not for amateurs, and as the AT&T experience showed, amateurs come in all forms. The worst of them are the people who are supposed to be the experts. When they have it wrong, everyone suffers. But fortunately, you do have the right map, right here in your hands.

If you apply the rules and follow the advice I've given you in this book, you will realize terrific results in your life through the use of cartoons. They truly are little pieces of magic.

"Here, try these."   *"Perfect!"*

Chapter Sixteen

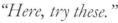

Cartooning resources

I want to congratulate you. By reading this book and arriving at this chapter, you now know far more than those "experts" ever did about the use of cartoons in all sorts of missions in your life and career. You understand what goes into creating a cartoon that is effective. You understand how to target the cartoon based on its underlying truth, rather than focusing on the surface and trying to inject your brand into it, like amateurs do. You're forearmed with knowledge that took thirty years and millions of dollars worth of double-blind testing to compile and perfect.

And now you're probably anxious to put this new expertise to use. I have assembled a list of resources on the following pages to help you incorporate not only cartoons, but all of the expertise you've read about in this book, into your campaigns and projects. This list is likely to expand as we open new partnerships and new tools for your use, so I invite you to visit the CartoonLink.com site often to see what's new -- or you can join CartoonLink Members™ , a club that includes a monthly newsletter and webinar, and an unlimited supply of one-at-a-time cartoon e-cards.

CartoonLink (www.CartoonLink.com)

CartoonLink is my company, and it's built around serving all of the uses and missions described in this book. Most of what we do is based on becoming a member of various marketing programs that include an allowance of campaign pieces each month, plus training and coaching by me and my staff. Some programs even allow you to reserve your market exclusively, so your competitors don't get to use specific Cartoon-Link programs in your area. All of our programs are designed around the use of personalized cartoons only. The CartoonLink team includes many of the cartoonists I have introduced to you in the book, most of whom are published regularly in *The New Yorker* and other national magazines.

CartoonLink e-Mail Marketer Program: This program is set up to allow you to use our personalized cartoons in monthly e-mail campaigns using your ConstantContact, iContact, Lyris or other white-listed e-mail delivery accounts. The program includes various HTML templates you can use to drop in your choice of cartoon, your message, logo, etc. to quickly and easily create custom monthly e-mail campaigns. Or use the cartoons in your own campaign designs, as a way to boost open rates and engagement in your message. Membership includes monthly training and coaching sessions with me via webinar.

CartoonLink BigBoards™: Contact campaigns are my favorite use of cartoons. Just one well-placed BigBoard can change the course of your business, by opening the door to a whole new level of access. It's a world where you're suddenly dealing with CEOs, making bigger sales, and pulling off ROI figures so high they almost don't make sense. Our Cartoon-Link BigBoard Program includes custom creative help, an allowance of ten or more BigBoard campaigns each month plus a monthly training/coaching session with me via webinar.

CartoonLink BigBoards™ Enterprise: If you have a large sales force and want to formulate a BigBoard program for use across your entire staff, we will work with you to create a custom program. Elements may include custom creative of your BigBoards for numerous missions, exclusive webinar-based training and coaching and of course, production and delivery of the BigBoards themselves.

CartoonLink Postcard Program: If sending monthly postcards through the mail is your preference, this program is for you. It includes a monthly allowance of postcards as part of your membership fee, as well as simple templates for creating your campaigns. Also included is a monthly training and coaching session with me via webinar.

CartoonLink Presentations: No monthly membership required, just license usage of our personalized cartoons for your PowerPoint presentations whenever you need them, at a very reasonable cost.

CartoonLink Members™: Become a member of the CartoonLink site to receive our monthly newsletter, free e-cards featuring our personalized cartoons with your logo or personal identity, and a monthly webinar with me or my staff. This is perfect if you want to use the power of cartoons in your projects without using the programs above, but still gain the benefit of my experience.

Custom assignments: I and my team are always available for custom assignments for larger marketers. We do this on a completely individual basis, with flexible terms to fit your requirements. This is not the way to find yourself a bargain, however, because it is an expensive process to develop a custom campaign from scratch. If a bargain is what you're looking for, consider one of the membership programs above.

Visit us at CartoonLink.com for more information or to join any of our programs.

AmazingMail/PremiumPostcard

The CartoonLink programs are based on monthly membership and volume, but certainly there are times when you just want to send a card or two, or maybe thousands when you need them. Then AmazingMail or PremiumPostcard are for you. They have a selection of some of the top personalized cartoons from the CartoonLink image bank and an amazingly simple on-line ordering process that allows you to build your postcard piece in minutes. Whether you order thousands at a time or just one postcard, it goes out the next day. PremiumPostcard is their resident brand on the U.S. Postal Service Web site. You can visit USPS.com to locate the PremiumPostcard portal and use the same interface, and launch a salvo of one or many postcards, which all mail the next day. Both offer a variety of postcard sizes and fold-over formats.

Visit them at AmazingMail.com, PremiumPostcard.com or on USPS.com, or phone them toll-free at 866-913-1482.

The Cartoon Bank

The Cartoon Bank has been mentioned throughout this book. Founded by Bob Mankoff, Cartoon Editor of *The New Yorker*, it is the place to find non-personalized cartoons on virtually any subject. With nearly 70,000 cartoons actually published in *The New Yorker* and another 80,000 that were not, you can find cartoons on virtually any topic and license them for various uses or purchase them on t-shirts and mugs. The shop lists many other products too numerous to mention, including calendars, note cards, covers, shower curtains and more. You can even buy original drawings that have appeared in the magazine. So what do you do with all of this? Non-personalized cartoons are terrific devices for amplifying a point; sending a cartoon to a prospective employer, customer or someone socially will get you noticed and open doors. Many of their items make wonderful gifts, personal or for business. And if you need non-personalized cartoons for a presentation, this is the place to go.

Visit the Cartoon Bank on-line at www.CartoonBank.com or call toll-free (U.S only), 1-800-897-TOON (8666).

Successories

Successories is best known for its series of inspirational posters featuring photography, for example, of a team rowing a shell with the headline, "Teamwork" below -- and many similar kinds of messages. These are found in offices around the world, their messages meant to inspire greater teamwork, productivity and morale. They have just launched a new line of framed posters in their "SOHO" section that includes a series of cartoons by Arnie Levin, Mick Stevens, Leo Cullum and me. You can't personalize or change the captions, but you can include your own personal message below the cartoon, which makes them perfect gifts to say, "Thank you," "Looking forward to working with you," "I hope I get the job" or virtually anything else you want to say. They can be shipped directly to any address in the U.S. or internationally.

Visit Successories at www.Successories.com/soho or call toll-free (U.S. only) 1-800-535-2773.

Sandler Training

Like most business owners, what I really do for a living is sell. And like most people who sell, while I enjoy meeting people, I find the process itself often less productive than I would like. Fortunately, I discovered Sandler Training. Their system turns the selling dynamic completely around so that your meetings become far more powerful and successful. Sales take less time, because you have a system for quickly discovering what the prospect needs and whether it's worth your time. Sandler is a network of 250 franchised offices worldwide, serving more than 100,000 businesses. And they are in the process of becoming a partner and reseller of our BigBoards program, which makes a very powerful combination. CartoonLink Big-Boards can open doors you could only dream of and Sandler's training will ensure that every meeting reaches its maximum potential. It is a sure-fire growth strategy for your business, or for your sales career.

Find your nearest Sandler Training office by visiting www.sandler.com or call 410-653-1993.

WSI

WSI is another worldwide franchise and partner. Their network of more than 2,000 Internet Marketing Consultants provide services ranging from site design and hosting to search marketing, e-mail marketing and more, throughout the world. They are also resellers of our CartoonLink programs. So why would you want to work with a reseller? Your WSI consultant will help you to integrate our tools into your overall Internet marketing program. There is no impact on pricing of our services, so the value is in the individual attention you'll receive, as well as global perspective of your marketing plan and their deep resources for all sorts of Internet marketing services no local designer or agency can provide.

Locate your nearest WSI Internet Consultant by visiting www.wsicorporate.com, call them toll-free in the U.S. or Canada at 1-888-678-7588. From the U.K., you can reach them at 0808-234-6105, or from anywhere else in the world, call their Toronto headquarters at +905-678-7588.

The Punch Cartoon Library

Punch was a great British humor magazine that started publication in 1841 and unfortunately, ceased in 2002. During that period, the magazine published over 500,000 cartoons by some of the world's finest cartoonists. Its stock of cartoons is not only enormous, it is historic, spanning the American Civil

War, both World Wars, the dawn of aviation and the moon missions, the invention of television and radio -- essentially everything leading to what we know today as our modern culture. While the Punch Cartoon Library has not digitized the entire series, they do make a selection of images available for licenses and as gifts. Visit them on the Web at www.punchcartoons. com or call +44 (0)207 576 9497.

CartoonStock

CartoonStock is another company based in the U.K. Their repository hosts more than 200,000 gag cartoons by more than 600 cartoonists from around the world, all of which are available for licensing and in the form of various gift items. Visit CartoonStock.com or call them toll-free in the U.S. at 888-880-8357, or their U.K. headquarters at +44 1225 789600.

Cloud2You on Salesforce

If you use Salesforce.com as your CRM and sales automation platform, you're in for a treat. Cloud2You is an Appexchange plug-in solution that allows you to send postcards and greeting cards bearing our CartoonLink personalized cartoons. What's amazing is that you can send these cards, one at a time or a campaign of thousands, all from an easy to use interface within your Salesforce dashboard, and it all goes out the next business day. Also amazing: the handwritten font that makes each card look like you sat down and wrote it out yourself, by hand. To plug into the Cloud2You service, you'll have to be a Salesforce account holder, and you can easily set it up from the business apps section.

Galleries

Original art pieces by magazine single-panel gag cartoonists make spectacular gifts and are suprisingly affordable, compared to the inflated prices of animation cells and comic book art. Try these sources as a starting point for your search:

Albert Moy Gallery, albertmoy.com, 718-225-3261
Heritage Auction Galleries, www.ha.com, 800-872-6467
The New Yorker Store, newyorkerstore.com, 877-408-4269

For updates on resources, visit CartoonLink.com

by Stu Heinecke © CartoonLink, Inc.

Chapter Seventeen

Let's keep in touch

Now that we gotten to know each other, I'd like to stay in touch. I think you will find it useful and profitable and I want to help foster as many success stories as possible. The best way to do that is to join one of our CartoonLink programs, by visiting CartoonLink.com. Whether you're ready to join one of our programs or not, you can participate with us as an affiliate, or as a link partner by displaying my monthly cartoon feature on your site. And finally, I have set aside a few free downloads to thank you for buying this book.

Share your success story

If you have experienced a success story resulting from the use of a cartoon, whether based on your reading of this book or not, I would love to hear from you and your story could end up in my next book. As you may recall, I have already heard a number of positive stories concerning the use of cartoons, and have shared them in this book. Andrew Fowler enlightened us with his very successful use of cartoons in social media. Jay Marks did the same by sharing stories and tips from his use of cartoons in PowerPoint and printed presentations. And I would love to include your stories as well, in future writings.

The best way to get in touch with me is through the CartoonLink site.

Spread the word

If you like what you've read, please help us spread the word. I don't have the ability to create reciprocal links, but if my teachings about the use of cartoons is something you believe in, something that resonates with you, I would greatly appreciate a link to the CartoonLink site as a marketing resource to your site visitors.

But you don't have place links without something in return, because as a member of our link partner program, you can include my monthly cartoon feature on your site simply in exchange for a set of links

If you have a blog or just like to comment in blogs, a favorable mention there would also be greatly appreciated. In fact, if you contact us first, we will be happy to provide a link to a specific cartoon to help add visual flash to the entry.

I encourage you to visit the CartoonLink site often, register or join one of our programs. We are constantly looking for ways to use our cartoons to provide new value to marketers and other users, and that is how you'll be able to participate in new programs as they come out.

Are you a potential strategic partner? We're always looking for ways to leverage our cartoons and programs with partners who can help us reach larger audiences and sales channels. White listed e-mail services, direct marketing, sales promotion, corporate gift companies are of immediate interest to us. Use our "Contact Us" link on the CartoonLink site to get in touch and let's see what develops.

I am also available as a speaker or for press interviews, again, via the "Contact Us" link on the CartoonLink site.

Become an affiliate

Whether your site attracts an audience of marketers, sales professionals, job seekers, speakers or virtually anyone else, we probably have a program that's right for your site visitors. You can participate with us as an affiliate and earn 50% of the first month's revenue from any membership sold through your efforts. Sign up at CartoonLink.com/affiliates. Review and approval of your site is required.

Free downloads

To thank you for purchasing this book, I have reserved a gift for you. The "StuHeinecke Dingbats" font, which is the source of the tiny spot illustrations found throughout the book, is available for free download at CartoonLink.com/claim_font. To claim your gift, you will need the receipt number from your book purchase.

Acknowledgements

It seems everyone has a book they plan to write sometime in their lives. This is my first, and it was a vivid reminder of the generous help I have received from the many people who have supported me, who took a chance on my crazy ideas and the people who have given me a great deal of encouragement, right on through the writing of this book.

I have already thanked my family for their support, while I worked slavishly at the computer at all hours, pushing to finish this book, but it bears repeating. I stayed up too late far too much, and spent too much time away from you. I can't thank my family enough for their kind and loving support throughout this writing.

A great debt of gratitude is owed to Lee Lorenz and Bob Mankoff, the successive Cartoon Editors at *The New Yorker* who helped me immensely in various ways, particularly with introductions to other cartoonists. Without their help, I would not have had this crazy career mixing marketing, science and cartooning.

I am especially grateful to Bob Mankoff for participating in this book, as the writer of one of the forewords. Bob is a historic figure in cartooning, having shaped and nurtured the current generation of top magazine gag cartoonists. He is an undisputed authority on the subject of humor and its effects, and a kindred spirit in the quest to quantify those effects. I am eternally grateful for his help with this book.

I met Bruce Seidman, President of Sandler Training, in the way you might expect after reading this book. I sent him a BigBoard. We have only known each other for about eight months, but we have fostered an exciting, collaborative relationship in that time. It was through his support that we were able to launch some of the tests of the BigBoards system that have produced such extraordinary results. Part of that stems from the BigBoards, but a lot of that success undoubtedly comes as a result of the superb training and expert staff found throughout the Sandler franchise family. I gratefully acknowledge Bruce's generous support with the BigBoard program and for his foreword in this book.

What would a book about cartooning be without cartoons? I'm so fortunate to be involved in such an amazing profession, because there is a built-in feeling of support among cartoonists, which showed up in a big way in the making of this book. Thank you Arnie Levin, Gahan Wilson, Bob Mankoff, Lee Lorenz, Matt Diffee, Mick Stevens and Anne Gibbons, for your generous support in allowing me to include your work in this book. A posthumous thank-you goes out to Leo Cullum, Eldon Dedini and Michael Ffolkes for your life-changing and awe-inspiring tutelage in the art of cartooning and of life. And although I don't know them (yet), thank you, Ed and Roz for your contributions to the art form of cartooning and for your drawings in this book.

Some of the cartoons appear in these pages also in part thanks to the Cartoon Bank and the Punch Cartoon Library. Both organizations are referenced in Chapter 16 and I heartily recommend them for their historic collections of cartoons, which are available for use in your campaigns.

This book relies heavily on a very unique body of test history, which would not have existed without the vision of the many marketers who took a chance and invested in tests of my humor-based approach to direct marketing. Even though the "experts" dismissed the use of humor, these courageous and visionary souls forged ahead, and we're left with a treasure of market-tested techniques for the use of cartoons as a result. So a big thank-you goes out to Lawrence Freeman, Susan Allyn, Steve Forbes, Michele Jehle, Allison Ackerman, Kim Malcolm, Michael Marion, Joan Wolf-Wooley, Nancy Lambert, Bob Cohn, Holly Spect, Brian Wolfe, Pat Servidea, Mark Stanich, Bobbi Gutman, Charles Mast, Peter Savage, Jose Perez, Curt Baker, Mary Lindewirth, Don Liebling, Frances Davis, Mike Nass, Dave Kelly, Blair Bergstrom, Walter Rosenthal, Howard Niebart, Joanne Guralnick, Jeff Fisher, Chris Wilkes, Laura Zandi, Michael Loeb, Nicola Wodlinger, Ilene Cohen, Tom Augeri, Suzanne Nicholas, Roni Stein, Michele Oram, Margaret Lorczak, Liberta Abbondante, Mark Davila, Allen Tacket, Julie Witsken, Barbara Eskin, Jon Spoelstra, Richard Erb, Cheryl Lovinsky, Kimberly Hickerson-Luhn, Jennifer Bielat, Debbie Huml and Christopher Purcell. I have surely left out many I should have remembered and if I missed you, you're still part of the group that made a big difference to direct marketing and beyond and I thank you.

When you're bucking the advice of industry experts, it is helpful to have an influential voice on your side. I have always found that in Denny and Peggy Hatch. In the early years, Denny was editor and publisher of *Target Marketing Magazine* and the highly-influential newsletter, *Who's Mailing What?* From his powerful pulpit, Denny would sometimes be the lone voice in the industry, other than my own, saying, hey wait a minute, humor does make sense. His wife Peggy, who is now Group President of North American Publishing, publishers of *Target Marketing* and fifteen other advertising and direct marketing oriented magazines, has also been an ardent supporter, and I thank them both for a career-long support that continues to this day.

I have mentioned elsewhere in this book how much I enjoy one particular use of cartoons, contact campaigns. This is so much fun, reaching out to people I would otherwise have no business contacting, but somehow, cartoons have been my passport. For their generous and kind responses to my crazy contact campaigns, which have formed part of the basis for this book, I would like to thank in particular, Ken Chenault, CEO of American Express, Steve Forbes, Editor and Publisher of *Forbes Magazine*, Governor Pete Wilson and Williams-Sonoma CMO Pat Connolly.

There is one celebrity I need to single out, someone whose response turned into a long-time friendship and collaboration: Syndicated radio and television personality Rick Dees. When Rick received my original cartoon postcard, he called and invited me to visit his studio, where we decided I would create his Christmas cards from then on. That was more than twenty years ago and we're still collaborating on those yearly holiday cards, in part as a way to remain visible to his base of celebrity friends and interview contacts. Rick is a special guy who knows more about humor than I ever will, and I thank him for all the years of collaboration and friendship, which have also contributed to the concepts contained in this book.

There have been a number of people whom I have admired simply for the way they think and strategize. *Guerrilla Marketing* author Jay Conrad Levinson, marketing gurus Dan Kennedy and Bill Glazer, sales guru Mac Macintosh and others have not only fascinated me with their views on marketing and sales strategy, they helped me change the way I do business. I like to think of myself as an honorary guerrilla marketer and Jay Levinson's acknowledgement of that status in various forms has meant a great deal to me throughout my career. Dan and Bill introduced me to several concepts that are now key components of my business, including the continuity approach to marketing programs. This has provided a framework for maximizing my working relationships with my client base. For your ingenious thinking and its contribution to the way I do business -- and to this book -- I thank you all.

Those continuity programs have also provided plenty of learning, which has been applied to this book. I would like to thank some of the pioneering business owners and marketers who participated in pilot programs and who keep the spirit of testing and learning alive in our CartoonLink marketing programs. A big "thank you" goes out to Gregg Wallick, Todd Nathan, Dennis Olson, Tom Shuster, Barry Kindt, Elliot McKean, Jim Lampkin, Rod Miller, Bill Logan, Rick Cunningham,

Ralph Blake, Craig Garey, Dave Homerding, Tom French, Jim Fox, Kris and Steve Anstandig, Nick Lyon, Holly Johnson, Chip Purcell, Dave Cleary, Kelly Steele, Brett Fogle and Mike Keating.

Our continuity marketing programs later gained great extension through their introduction to entire franchise and sales networks, which furthered the test experience body for this book. For their contributions to making that happen, I thank Ron MacArthur, Dan Monaughan, Doug Schust, Frank Milner, Stephen Barron and Peter Feigenbaum.

None of this would have happened if I hadn't gained experience right out of college, as marketing manager for Crest Steel in Wilmington, California. It was a terrific family of people to work with, but Rich Mangone was the standout for me. He was my boss, mentor and friend, who encouraged me to push forward with my original use of cartoons in marketing, in their weekly mail campaign. That is what launched the ship and I thank him for his kind guidance and friendship.

And for that crazy time in my life, when I suddenly found myself single and ready for adventure, who could have fit the description of the perfect friend and wingman but famed Hollywood director and photographer Jay Silverman? That year and a half or so that we haunted the restaurants and bars of L.A. were some of my favorite times ever as a bachelor. Little did we know those misadventures would later form the basis of a chapter in this book, but they did so magically. I laughed out loud throughout the writing of that chapter, recounting all of those terrific memories. I hope some of the readers of this book will be able to repeat a few of those stunts and find themselves the center of attraction in bars and restaurants throughout the world.

In the end, it is your friends and family who see you through an endeavor like this. I have thanked my family, but I also must extend my warmest thanks to good friends Ron Braley and Cherie Ware, whose encouragement throughout the years helped keep the dream of writing this book alive. They're the kind of friends I wish everyone could have.

About the Author

Stu Heinecke is one of the world's foremost experts on the use of cartoons in advertising, marketing and sales promotion, having blended cartooning and marketing for nearly thirty years.

He and his collaborators, including many of the cartoonists found in *The New Yorker*, have created numerous record-breaking campaigns for some of the world's biggest direct marketers, including Time, Inc., AT&T, *Forbes Magazine, Harvard Business Review*, GSK GlaxoSmithKline, Sandoz Pharmaceuticals and the NBA and NHL.

Throughout his career, Mr. Heinecke has battled many of the top "experts" in the direct marketing industry, all of whom claimed "humor does not work" in marketing and advertising. His 2010 nomination to the Direct Marketing Association's Hall of Fame came in recognition of his compelling body of work, which has proven beyond a shadow of a doubt that humor is extremely effective in those missions.

A prominent cartoonist whose work can be seen in countless marketing campaigns and occasionally in the pages of *The Wall Street Journal* and other publications, Mr. Heinecke is the President and Founder of Seattle-based CartoonLink, where he lives with his wife, three kids, two dobermans and a snake.

.

Testimonials

"Stu Heinecke hits the nail on the head as he tickles the funny bone with his incredibly insightful book, 'Drawing Attention.' I highly recommend it to all guerrilla marketers, in fact, to everyone who wants just a bit too much money."

Jay Conrad Levinson
The Father of Guerrilla Marketing
Author, "Guerrilla Marketing" series of books

"In the 35 years I've known Stu Heinecke, he's been direct marketing's odd man out. Pinning direct mailings to cartoons with the recipient's name personalized in the caption, Stu's work has been pilloried by the uppity elitist circle of advertising creatives—from David Ogilvy on down—who parrot the dictum that 'Humor never works in advertising.' Funnily enough it does—big time—but only if done right. Stu has created a blizzard of controls and generated zillions in revenue for myriad clients. In his chatty, informative 'Drawing Attention,' Stu—like a magician revealing his tricks—tells how he did it and how you can, too. Look for lotsa laffs and lotsa dough."

Denny Hatch
Author of *Million Dollar Mailings* and *The Secrets of Emotional Hot-Button Copywriting*, Editor and Publisher of *Denny Hatch's Business Common Sense*

"Not only was I unable to stop reading 'Drawing Attention' but I found it to be a highly detailed insight into the world of the cartoonist, as well as a good overview of marketing and business practice, psychology and sociology which transcends the endeavour of cartooning. Mr. Heinecke's enthusiasm and style makes it read like a self-help book!"

Andre Gailani
Punch Ltd.

"Stu, you and your cartoons have been an major part of our business development and branding efforts over the years. Our affiliation with CartoonLink can be tied back to millions of dollars worth of contracts over the years. Plus you are fun to work with, then again what would you expect from a 'Cartoon Guy.' Congratulations on your book!"

Gregg Wallick, President
Best Roofing

"Can you imagine the wonderful feeling of having Oprah or Arnold or Madonna say, 'I can't wait to get your Christmas card every year!' Well, it sounds like a dream, but it's a reality, thanks to my close friend and collaborator, Stu Heinecke. Stu's

personalized cartoon cards cut through the clutter like a hot knife through butter. His genius comes from tapping into the part of your brain that makes you giggle."

Rick Dees
Syndicated radio and TV personality

Through the blending his creative gift with his direct response brilliance, Stu has produced spectacular results that business owners can continue to take to the bank - day in and day out!"

Dan Monaughan
Co-Founder, WSI Internet